collected and edited by Susan L. Scott

STORIES IN MY NEIGHBOUR'S FAITH

NARRATIVES FROM WORLD RELIGIONS IN CANADA

United Church Publishing House

Toronto, Canada

Stories in My Neighbour's Faith:
Narratives from World Religions in Canada

The excerpt on pages 6–7 from *Becoming Human* by Jean Vanier © Jean Vanier and the Canadian Broadcasting Corporation, 1998. Published by the House of Anansi Press Ltd., Toronto. Reprinted with the permission of Stoddart Publishing Co. Limited, Don Mills, Ontario.

Care has been taken to trace ownership of copyright material contained in this text. The publisher will gratefully accept any information that will enable it to rectify any reference or credit in subsequent printings.

All biblical quotations, unless otherwise noted, are from the *New Revised Standard Version Bible*, copyright © 1989, by the Division of Christian Education of the National Council of the Churches of Christ in the United States of America. Used by permission.

Canadian Cataloguing in Publication Data

Main entry under title:

Stories in my neighbour's faith : narratives from world religions in Canada

ISBN 1-55134-100-X

1. Canada - Religion. 2. Religions. I. Scott, Susan L. (Susan Lorraine), 1955- .

BL2530.C3S76 1999	200'971	C99-930614-6

United Church Publishing House
3250 Bloor Street West, Suite 300
Etobicoke ON
Canada M8X 2Y4
416-231-5931
bookpub@uccan.org

Design, Editorial, and Production:
Department of Publishing and Graphics

Printed in Canada
5 4 3 2 1   03 02 01 00 99

A Project of the Interfaith Dialogue Committee

980392

CONTENTS

*The mind slows down and opens, and the
story goes under the skin and enters the
heart.*

Jon Kabat-Zinn

ACKNOWLEDGEMENTS

This book has come to fruition through the kindness of many people. Foremost are the contributors themselves, whose generous donations of time and effort made the project a success. To all who opened their doors, I offer my deepest gratitude; people's desire to participate in interfaith dialogue was overwhelming. Rita Joe's desire, however, was curtailed by illness. Selections from her award-winning *Song of Rita Joe: Autobiography of a Mi'kmaq Poet*, published by Ragweed Press, Charlottetown, Prince Edward Island, are used with permission of the publisher.

I am delighted to be able to thank Bruce Gregersen publicly. Bruce spearheaded the stories project and risked turning it over to a rather unconventional editor; without his determination and initiative, the book would never have seen the light of day. I would also very much like to thank the co-sponsor of the project, the *Multifaith Calendar*, editors David Spence and Charles Anderson, for patient, concrete support.

Many people made suggestions about contributors or facilitated contact. I'd like to thank the following for help along the way: Sheila Ayala at the Humanist Association of Canada; Barbara Bortz; Ellen Campbell, general secretary of the Canadian Unitarian Council; Ginny Freeman MacOwan; Norma Joseph; Celine Leduc; Leslie Menzies; Pratash Modi and Irena Upenicks from Toronto's Jain community; Kim Pate, executive director of the Canadian Association of Elizabeth Fry Societies; Bob Sinkewicz; and Sue Tennant, for setting me on the path.

For valuable insight into various traditions, I appreciate the guidance offered by Dolly Dastoor, president of FEZANA (Federation of Zoroastrian Associations of North America); the Baha'i Community of Canada; Jacques Langlais; Sajjan Singh Sidhu and Sidhu; and Julie Green of CBC, Goose Bay. I am especially indebted to Anthony Jenkinson for astute cultural analysis of Innu life, and to Yuri Kyssa, whose gifted translation of Russian proved indispensable. Finally, I would like to express my appreciation to all those who responded to the manuscript, particularly members of the Interfaith Committee. Heartfelt thanks also goes to the United Church Publishing House, which shepherded the book to completion, and to my husband, Ron Grimes. For technical assistance, moral support, and true companionship, he is second to none.

INTRODUCTION

*This [is] the secret of interfaith dialogue—not
that we seek to convert each other, but that
we help one another find what is meaningful in our own traditions.*

Amir Hussain, "Shannon's Song"

*No one remembers her name, but her story is
still remembered.*

Shirlee Smith, "I've Got Shoes, You've Got Shoes"

*Yet some people's stories can never be told.
There is no one left to tell them.*

Joyce Rappaport, "Every Person Has a Story"

Stories in My Neighbour's Faith gathers together sacred and personal
narratives from over twenty traditions across Canada. Like its
predecessor, *Faith in My Neighbour*, this book also invites people
to explore one another's worlds. The added beauty of stories,
however, is that they take us one step further, beyond description,
into hearts and minds, into the lives of men and women struggling
to become whole.

The anthology begins with the Torah creation account and ends
with an Innu *atanuken*. In between lie sutras, song, and scripture;
hagiography and fables; tales of heroes, prophets, and gods; and
meditations on the nature of the cosmos, on what is right and
wrong with the world. When these are combined with personal
reflections, two kinds of stories surface, one communal and

traditional, the other contemporary and personal. Dovetailing the two is what makes *Stories in My Neighbour's Faith* unique.

In the West religious stories typically find their way into writing and endure in a variety of forms such as scripture and spiritual autobiography. In many traditions, however, stories are not written at all. Storytelling is an ancient art that stands at the centre of traditions whose heritage is rooted in oral rather than recorded memory. Traditional storytellers do not just spin a good yarn; they embody crucial cultural and spiritual knowledge, the transmission of which may be carefully guarded. There are men's stories and women's stories, stories performed and stories ritualized. There are those that are bestowed only when someone is ready to receive them and that only certain individuals have the right to tell.

Whether performed or in print, storytelling is a powerful dynamic that gives voice to all aspects of existence. Stories enlighten and instruct; they anchor identity, entertain, and console. Rooted in the imagination, stories have the power to heal, to enchant, even to destroy. Like other sacred arts storytelling draws people together, illuminating fantastic scenarios and forbidden terrains. The abstract and obscure become accessible through stories. They bring religion to life.

Tapping this core of lived religion brings an added dimension to interfaith relations. Instead of talking about faith, we meet faithful people, and the grounds of our encounter shift from abstraction to intimacy. This move is by no means easy. A large number of faith communities and individuals across the country were invited to participate in the stories project; not all chose to do so. Those who did, however, took an active interest in weaving together traditional stories and personal reflections, a commitment that meant risking public disclosure of some very private experiences. That in itself took determination, and contributors matched that determination with an equal dose of creative energy. Some worked independently, while others submitted a variety of materials, ranging from poetry to journal excerpts, sermons, and articles. Those who were unable to donate written accounts kindly agreed to interviews. The voices that emerged through this process were every bit as textured as the varying sensibilities and points of view. Rather than homogenize these, I have tried to highlight people's strengths, whether they be oral, scholarly, or poetic. This freedom to experiment with form and to collaborate also made it possible to work with an eclectic group of people, all of whom graciously agreed to dialogue and revision and to answering endless inquiries.

From one standpoint it would have been easier to garner stories from seasoned writers, in which case we would have had an excellent overview of religious narratives and would still know little about the spiritual lives of so-called ordinary Canadians. The latter are so little known. Most works feature published authors; very few include voices from all walks of life. *Stories in My Neighbour's Faith* does just that. Educators, artists, elders, students, scholars, scientists, clergy, and community workers all offer narratives that are grounded both in their traditions and in their own lives. The contributors are by no means representative of their respective faiths, nor are their accounts always models of interfaith dialogue. They are, however, authentic portraits of women and men reaching out, sometimes across enormous cultural barriers, trying to speak and be heard.

When it comes to communicating across religious boundaries, there is no easy road; yet this very complexity underscores how richly textured lived religion actually is. "About the Contributors" reveals not only the range of traditions flourishing across the country but also the calibre of those committed to these paths. What we glimpse in this book, then, is a microcosm of storytelling in different traditions and a glimmer of the religious passion and imagination thriving on Canadian soil:

> *Out of the shock and pain at the sudden experience of the inexorable betrayal of all I held sacred, my heart broke open.*
>> "The Tragedy of Karbala"

> *Out of pure love for this young man's soul, I had consented in the dream to help him.*
>> "The Pepal Tree"

*I have survived as a dancer because of hope,
the aspiration that I share the dance.*
"Precious Knowledge, Sacred Dance"

When I paint, I live in my icon.
"Waiting for Morning: Artist and Icon"

For better or worse, religion is currently a term that alienates many people, especially those who associate it with institutionalized systems of belief. A preferred term these days is spirituality. Spirituality often refers to the experiential and to introspective or contemplative paths to a richer, more meaningful life. Personal stories usher us into that domain—a place that is hidden, private, yet the site of some of the most intense debate among world religions. Rigorous ascetic practices, meditation, and prayer are all rooted here, in hopes of transforming the inner person. Spiritual autobiography is an intimate portrayal of this interiority, yet historically much of what we have had access to are works by religious giants. Spiritual experiences of the average person are seldom gathered and explored. Portraits of children, too, are rare. Fortunately, a number of authors felt propelled back to childhood to recall their earliest spiritual awakenings:

*I was kneeling beside my mother on the
women's side of the sanctuary when somehow her nearness, the warmth of the sun
streaming through the high, simple windows, and the comforting drone of the
altesta's (bishop's) kindly voice...filled me
with a spirit of worship.*
"The Gift: Growing Up Mennonite"

Highly charged and emotionally nuanced, these childhood scenes are laden with sensual detail:

*And as they worked, I watched with great
intensity the movement of the hand-held
scythes and the falling sheaves of golden*

hay, following the rhythm of each movement
with my eyes.

"Danny's Toy Truck"

The dark side of childhood, its vagaries and threats, are plumbed as well:

I grew up in a fast, unstable lifestyle. I
watched my parents fight and drink and
separate.

"The Snake and the Stone"

I was ten when my mother was possessed by
a stranger God.

"Spirit Dance"

Moments like these that recall the vulnerability of children are reminders that spiritual awareness does not belong to adults alone. Yet how easy it is to dismiss such moments as insignificant in the grand scheme of things. By the same token, persons with remarkable spiritual qualities may be overlooked because they lack public voice or are confined by minority status. Then too, people who are estranged from their tradition or who keep to the periphery often have important—some would say prophetic—insights. Care has been taken to see that both marginal and mainstream perspectives find a home in this collection.

Spiritual masters in sacred scripture often
tell stories to reveal truths and to awaken
hearts. Jesus spoke in parables; Hasidic Jews
and Sufi teachers tell tales; Hindu scripture
is full of stories. Stories seem to awaken new
energies of love; they tell us great truths in
simple, personal terms and make us long for
light. Stories have a strange power of attrac-
tion. When we tell stories, we touch hearts. If
we talk about theories or speak about ideas,

5

> *the mind may assimilate them but the heart*
> *remains untouched.*
>
> Jean Vanier, *Becoming Human*

We live in a culture where religious experience is highly psychologized, and in our efforts to find a sophisticated vocabulary for interiority, we sometimes forget that the simplest words convey the most common and profound experiences. Buddhist sutras speak with unadorned clarity, as do Aboriginal legends and the gospel parables. Stories influence us at a deep level not because they may conjure the unexpected but because they evoke the utterly familiar. Fear of loss, for instance:

> *I was excited at the idea of making a home*
> *for my family in one of the loveliest, most*
> *secure parts of the world, but at the same*
> *time, I felt apprehensive as the time of depar-*
> *ture neared, full of doubt and a little sad.*
>
> "The Parsis and Their Sacred Fire"

Delicious scandal, perhaps:

> *Now here was a bad egg, a dishonourable*
> *man who had cheated his brother, Esau, out*
> *of his birthright.*
>
> "Walking the Riverbank"

Or the poignancy of human relationships:

> *He would read his shocking life out loud to*
> *me, and I would gaze out the window,*
> *watching cars go by, watching the snow fall,*
> *watching normal lives pass by.*
>
> "Every Person Has a Story"

> *And then the old man started to cry because*
> *he missed his son.*
>
> "*Kauatikumapeu*: The Man who Married a Caribou"

These hearken to a fundamental sense of what it means to be human—broken, longing, alive. From the rudest anecdote to the finest poetry, the religious imagination pools from basic words and elemental images. The inherent power of story is that it relies on the shared currency of everyday speech and common human experience; this book is designed with that in mind.

In addition, each selection is followed by a thumbnail sketch of that particular faith in the Canadian context or of some aspect of storytelling in that tradition. Since there are many fine resources on comparative religion, we have aimed for something else: a guide to some of the key concepts raised in the stories themselves. Look for ways in which each person's story resonates with his or her background. What, for instance, identifies Fredelle Brief's concerns with those of the larger Jewish community? What makes Brenda Acoose Morrison's prison memoir a searing cultural critique and not just an isolated incident? What historical circumstances colour each work, bringing certain issues to the fore?

Listen closely to authors' tones of voice. Watch for turns of phrase, habits of mind. Cultural and religious values are deeply embedded in our speech, and they spring forth as our most natural modes of expression. Consider how different traditions speak to one another through their stories. What interfaith issues appear, and how do they change when exposed in a different light? Amir Hussain, Leona Penner, Karen Laughlin, and Guru Raj Kaur Khalsa all write about losing someone they love. How do Muslim, Christian, Taoist, and Sikh stories prepare practitioners to face the inevitability of grief and death, what Karen Laughlin calls "the ultimate letting go"?

Again and again these stories show how interwoven religion is with ordinary life. The most mundane things are fraught with significance, everything from stars to stones to a boy's toy truck. When sacred story is combined with life story, one flows into the other; the two domains embrace. Consider the array of song, prayer, scripture, myth, and fable, even family history, throughout the book. The sheer breadth says something important about the repertoire of sacred narratives in different traditions and about what constitutes sacred.

What then makes a story sacred? Lying, cheating, pomp, and fraud abound in the tales that follow. The most popular myths are often so fabulous, fiction can hardly hold a candle to them; yet they contain complex psychic or communal truths. In "*Kauatikumapeu*: The Man Who Marries a Caribou," the unpretentious dignity of the Innu tale lures us into suspended disbelief, rendering questions about its literal truth irrelevant. What determines whether a story is regarded as sacred may be less content than context—how and why a story is told.

The one thread that persists is life, that and the plain hard work of becoming fully human. Religions call this work by different names: enlightenment, redemption, and so on. Yet even with profound differences between traditions, interreligious influence is pervasive. This is particularly true in a pluralistic society such as ours and nowhere clearer than in the stories themselves. Themes and images ricochet from one tale to another, and each time they appear, our grasp of them is enhanced. Hindu temples, African Shango, and the Muslim martyr, Husain, all appear in Rolph Fernandes' recollections of growing up Christian in Trinidad. Author Deo Kernahan, however, was reared on the island as Hindu, and we re-visit the same enchanting land with a different host. But Muhammad's grandson, Husain, is also the hero of "The Tragedy of Karbala," Zohra Husaini's passionate rendition of Husain's horrific martyrdom in the Arabian desert. Meanwhile, the distant call of Shango drums persists long into the night, driving the young Bernadette Charles into possession in the irrepressibly lyrical "Spirit Dance."

Several stories have recurring motifs that link together unrelated traditions. Imprisonment and freedom, for example, frame Heather Botting's "Children of the Gods":

> *I had walked the Wiccan path for decades*
> *when it led me beneath the razor-wire*
> *arbour surrounding the steel gates of*
> *William Head Institution, a medium-*
> *security penitentiary for men.*

We leave one prison only to plunge into another, in "The Snake and the Stone," Brenda Acoose Morrison's haunting tribute to survival and healing. "Danny's Toy Truck" finds Louis Cormier trapped in the church confessional, and in "The Gift" Leona Penner recalls prayers for Mennonite youth in conscientious objector–camps during the war. The same motif, which threads its way through "Waiting for Morning" by Tatiana Vartanova, who was imprisoned by the KGB, resurfaces in Shirlee Smith's homage to her slave ancestors:

> *I was told the story by my mother, Myrtle,*
> *and it was the fuel that started the fire*
> *burning within me—the yearning to con-*
> *tinue my great-grandfather's journey to the*
> *heaven of freedom and equality for "all*
> *God's chillun." Deep in my soul I knew that*
> *this was no mere dream. I always believed*
> *that the oneness of humankind would some*
> *day be a reality.*
>
> "'I've Got Shoes, You've Got Shoes':
> Journeying to Freedom"

Just as crossover occurs between religious traditions, so too it connects our metaphors and images, the languages we speak. Deeply influenced by one another's symbols and myths, our imaginations are, in some sense, already peopled with one another's stories.

Every place has its lore. Canada is a vast land, teeming with myths reaching far back in time. Canada was a storied landscape long before Europeans arrived. For centuries, however, Christian stories have largely shaped our history and culture. Now that dominance is changing as other faiths introduce new perspectives and challenges.

Buddhism, for instance, is the fastest growing religion in North America. Both Buddhist authors in this collection searched for an authentic spiritual practice, free from the restrictive dogma they felt they had inherited from their Christian upbringing. Their frankness drives home the fact that religions fail as well as inspire, that they can be every bit as oppressive as liberating. What is liberating is the desire for dialogue and renewal, the hope for mutual transformation. Now, as never before, there is a place for dissenters and seekers, and for the likes of Ann Brennan, whose

Christian heritage is enriched by spiritual forces that pre-date the church by millennia:

> I need no altar
> Nor church spire
> For I have
> Blue sky overhead
> for my mantle
>
> "Journey to the Goddess"

For others, however, one religious orientation is as trying as the next. So we meet the skeptic, who prefers a society shaped by secular, rather than religious, ideals. Of course, this position isn't problem-free either, as we see in "Helen and Humanism," where David Lawson arrives at "a pointed re-evaluation of cultural assumptions [he] had long taken for granted." Vastupal Parikh's trenchant essay on Jainism is also marked by a pronounced shift, as the classically trained scientist runs headlong into the very thing he had once so cogently dismissed:

> *I had very little understanding of the reli-*
> *gious and ethical principles that had shaped*
> *my life. Certainly, I was a skeptic as far as*
> *religious faith was concerned, and since*
> *most religions demand belief (a form of*
> *blind faith, as far as I was concerned),*
> *religion had no validity in my life.*
>
> "Jainism: Promise of a Peaceful
> Twenty-first Century"

There is risk in attending to one's own story—the risk that comes with self-knowledge. No longer cushioned by abstract ideals, we come face to face with our own limitations and are finally freed to embrace change.

This emphasis on transformation is characteristic of sacred stories, which often contain powerful messages that urge the listener to act. "Walking by the Riverbank" probes the ethical dilemma of a Hebrew patriarch, and the fables in "The Donkey and the Jackal" are rife with moral and political blunders. Sacred stories are not meant as pure distractions. There are those that entertain, but there are also those that outrage and offend. The prophetic power of trickster tales, for example, provokes criticism by subverting the status quo.

Culture is thickly encoded in stories and in how they are told, which is why suppressing stories amounts to a kind of cultural annihilation. Aboriginal accounts, in particular, speak to this threat. When Rita Joe landed in residential school, she suddenly found herself subject to authorities who disdained her Mi'kmaq ways. Brenda Acoose Morrison suffered similar alienation from her roots. Not surprisingly, both women's accounts focus on the healing that is possible only when one's rightful heritage is restored. Devalued stories imply a people in danger, a culture ruptured and excluded from power or recognition. Matnen Benuen says what she most wants others to know about are Innu stories, so that "people [will] learn them and pass them on. Old stories are disappearing; no one tells them anymore."

Soonoo Engineer's moving portrayal of her Parsi ancestors' devout persistence in exile implies there is a collective responsibility for attending to communal stories. Sacred stories are among the most treasured symbols of cultural and religious identity. Fidelity to them is fidelity to one's origins and ancestors, to the future of the faith. The same is true for Holocaust stories. While they may be fast becoming a genre, it is easy to forget that not long ago these harrowing accounts were shrouded in silence. The history of the Holocaust is crucial to the theology and self-understanding of the Jewish people, and its preservation has itself become a sacred charge. Fredelle Brief and Joyce Rappaport both invite the memories of Holocaust survivors into the shelter of their own lives. Because they do so, private traumas are shouldered by collective awareness, borne by others long after the sufferers can no longer speak for themselves. Far from being merely individualistic, then, the most intimate narratives can inform the historical record, shaping meaning and identity for generations to come.

Stories tether the present to the past and imagination to memory. They map our views of what has gone before and our vision of what lies ahead. Stories alight unexpectedly, arresting us with bold, fleeting impressions, nourishing us for the journey ahead.

Telling and receiving stories invite us beyond dialogue to relationship, where the grip of isolation and the silence imposed by erasure are broken at last. In telling, we offer; through listening, we receive and allow ourselves to be moved by what we hear. Listening allows a story to return to its raconteur transformed, as gift.

May you welcome your neighbours' stories and prepare to voyage to their worlds. Some terrains are alluring, some remote, some as familiar as dreams. I have been a privileged companion to some remarkable travellers. Now the privilege falls to you.

Susan L. Scott,
Waterloo, Ontario

LISTENING AMONG THE STARS

You, the reader, and I, the storyteller are strangers. It is hard for me to tell you a story when I cannot see your face. Pretend with me for a while that we both just missed a train and are waiting together in the coffee shop. We strike up an idle conversation that moves eventually into explanations about how the world seems to work. Could I begin with how I look at myself?

I am a Jewish woman. My life takes meaning and winds around stories in two time frames: biblical and historical. When I was a little girl, I loved to watch the stars at night from my bedroom window. Although I was always struck by the rich complexity of the day-lit world around me, from the varieties of insects, birds, flowers, and trees to the changing shapes of the clouds and colours in the morning and evening sky, it was the stars and the heavens that held the greatest mystery for me. I could see them, but I could not touch them. As a child I thought that if I only looked hard enough, I would be able to see an image of God.

> *In the beginning of God's creating the heavens and the earth—when the earth was bewilderment and void with darkness over the surface of the deep and the breath of God was hovering upon the surface of the waters—God said "let there be light" and there was light. God saw that the light was good, and God separated between the light and the darkness. God called to the light: "Day" and to the darkness He called "Night." And there was evening and there was morning, one day.*
>
> Genesis 1:1*

This English translation of the Hebrew text begins the Torah, the source of the Jewish people's knowledge of the relationship between God and humankind. God is telling Moses the story. We wonder why God called the whole of creation into being and what God expects of us. We look for answers in the rest of the Torah and in the centuries of learned commentary on the Torah. When I listen to the Torah, I am listening as part of the Jewish people. My people are the "we" and the "us" in my story.

In the Torah stories God speaks to some of us directly. Sometimes, God challenges us by asking us to make decisions on faith alone. For example, he asked Abraham to leave his father's home and protection and move to an unknown land, which would belong to him and his descendants in perpetuity. That land is Israel. God also asks us difficult questions. "Where are you?" was the first question God posed to Adam. God asks that question of our biblical ancestors regularly in the Torah. As faithful Jews we must live our lives so conscious of our moral location that we could answer that question immediately. The events in the Torah took place long ago, and although our sense of wonder at the natural world today is diminished by many modern distractions, the biblical question still persists.

The Stone Edition Tanach, Nossan Scherman, Yaakov Blinder, Avie Gold, and Meir Zlotowitz. Brooklyn, NY: Mesorah Publications Limited, 1996.

Many Jews have asked the question "Where are You?" of God as well. The Holocaust is a modern catastrophe in contemporary Jewish history. Many Jews wonder where God was, when they hear the stories from those who survived the Holocaust.

These personal stories of people who lived through the Holocaust drew me into interfaith dialogue. I have read academic texts that rely on documentation to describe events leading to the murder of six million Jewish people during World War II, but I learn piercing moral information from the personal anecdotes of witnesses and survivors. They speak of their experience of the Holocaust as a series of irrational events.

My friend, Abe, was a child survivor of the Holocaust. I will share Abe's story with you because it tells me that human decency can be expressed in small, undramatic ways with great effect. Abe was a nine-year-old boy in a Jewish family in rural Poland when the German army invaded. His parents told him to leave the family home and run for his life, before they were taken to the death camps. Abe, who had fair hair and did not "look Jewish," found occasional work as a farmer's helper. One day a farmer asked Abe to bring produce demanded by the German army to a central collection point in the village. The produce collector was a local villager whom Abe recognized. Abe was carrying grain and feared that if he turned and ran away, he would be more conspicuous. He tied a cloth around his cheeks as though he had a toothache and plunked down the grain in front of the villager, avoiding any eye contact. The grain was accepted without incident. Abe lived out the rest of the war in the woods with other Jewish children and when he could find work, helping on local farms for food.

When the war was over, Abe saw the same local villager who had collected the produce for the Germans on the ship that brought them both to Canada. Abe recalled that awful day when he feared that the villager would recognize him. The man told Abe that he had recognized him but had chosen not to disclose to the German soldier that Abe was a Jew. That villager's moral choice saved Abe's life. Abe alone of all his family survived. He married and had children but, like many survivors of the Holocaust, died suddenly when he was a relatively young man.

There is a well-known Jewish legend that God so values compassionate, righteous people that there are always at least thirty-six such people alive somewhere in this world. When one compassionate, righteous person dies, another takes his or her place. The legend explains to us that it is for their sake that life as we know it continues. These people do not know who they are. Some are mild-mannered and others are fierce. Some are gifted intellectually or physically or spiritually, and others of these holy ones are just ordinary people. Since I was a little girl, I have been searching for those unique people who hear God's voice and are animated by what they hear.

When I was a little girl, I thought that I too would be able to hear God's voice in my life, just as my biblical ancestors did, if only I listened carefully. Now I think that those compassionate, righteous people function to make God's presence in the world more accessible to us all. For me as an adult they are more illuminating of God's closeness among us than all the stars in creation. I keep listening for one of the thirty-six in everyone I meet.

I see the train is coming. Could we sit together on the journey so that you might tell me about yourself and how you think the world works?

Fredelle Brief
Toronto, Ontario

"Do not do unto others what is hateful to you, all the rest is commentary" is an excellent summation of the heart of the Jewish understanding of what God wants of the Jewish people. Although modern Jews think of themselves as individuals with a variety of approaches, from traditional to secular, Jews also consider themselves part of a people who remember engagement with God from the time of Abraham and Sarah.

This sense of being a people has several dimensions. Jews believe God speaks to them both as individuals and as a people; they share a profound history back through time to the Torah and identify with biblical ancestors. At the same time, Jews also identify with the rest of the Jewish community elsewhere in the world;

hence the feeling of family. Yet another dimension is how Jews understand the future. Although individual lives are circumscribed by birth and death, souls return to God whence they came. In the future, all will be joined together in the world to come.

Two other world religions share their beginnings in Jewish history and have gone on to develop their own unique approaches. Yet the Judaism that began in the Bible has continued as a living religion to this day. Throughout history adherents of Christianity and Islam have sought to convert Jews, arguing that the Jewish people misunderstand what God wants from them and that Christians or Muslims have the answer. As a result, Jewish relations with Christians and Muslims have been strained to violence, and this too has shaped Jewish identity profoundly.

Through interfaith dialogue Jews, along with Christians and Muslims, are beginning to address these historical and contemporary challenges, and storytelling is an important part of that dialogue. Stories show how each of us is animated by our own faith-based values. Peace comes from listening with our whole hearts to one another's stories.

THE GIFT:
Growing Up Mennonite

For me, growing up in the close confines of a rural Russian Mennonite community in the heart of the flood plains of southern Manitoba, life and faith were inseparable. In fact, they seemed all of a piece: the food, the farm, the fun, the faith, the fellowship, even the feuding and fracturing. All these simply ebbed and flowed around me like the Morris River, which meandered through our pasture and spilled over its banks in spring.

For the most part, the community, like the river, was peaceful and life-giving. But now and then, as pressures relating to work and worship mounted, various groups and fissions would burst through communal boundaries—much like the backed-up waters of the great Red River, which flooded the narrow channels of our own little river—in search of freer, purer land.

And when that happened, there would be some mopping up to do before things flowed harmoniously again.

However, even though this integrated way of life was community-oriented, Mennonite emphasis on adult believers' baptism encouraged everyone to make a personal decision regarding the faith. This decision was reached after the "age of accountability," usually sometime during the teenage years. And though this emphasis on a personalized faith may have contributed to the fracturing and splintering—itself a part of European-rooted Mennonite history—it also gave people the opportunity to search out their own particular spiritual stepping stones in the river of faith.

Looking back on my own spiritual pilgrimage, I remember a sacred text that helped to ground me in my faith and that was passed on to me by my mother—the following letter by an elderly Apostle Paul for his spiritual child:

> To Timothy, my beloved child…I am grateful to God—
> whom I worship with a clear conscience, as my
> ancestors did—when I remember you constantly in my
> prayers…I am reminded of your sincere faith, a faith
> that lived first in your grandmother Lois and your
> mother Eunice and now, I am sure, lives in you. For
> this reason, I remind you to rekindle the gift of God
> that is within you through the laying on of my hands;
> for God did not give us a spirit of cowardice, but
> rather a spirit of power and of love and of self-
> discipline…continue in what you have learned and
> firmly believed, knowing from whom you learned it,
> and how from childhood you have known the sacred
> writings that are able to instruct you for salvation
> through faith in Christ Jesus…so that everyone who
> belongs to God may be proficient, equipped for every
> good work.
>
> II Timothy 1:2–7; 3:14–17

The main stepping stone, or rather rock, of my personal faith was the loving home into which I was welcomed at birth. The fifth child in a family of eleven, I was born at home during World War II in what used to be my paternal grandparents' house in Rosenhoff, Manitoba. My parents, Canadian-born, of Dutch–German, Russian Mennonite descent, were poor but very proud of their large family. Often my father would quote Psalm 127:5, "Happy is the man who has his quiver full of [children]." And like her namesake, Mary, the mother of Jesus, my own mother treasured and pondered in her heart all the events and details that surrounded the births of each of her eleven children.

To this day she is concerned that my premature birth and resulting calcium deficiency during early infancy had to do with the war-related stresses she experienced during pregnancy. Recently she told me again that she had often been anxious during those years not so much because of food shortages ("We always had enough to eat, and I was able to give some of our ration coupons to others who needed them"), but because of the tragedy that was unfolding in Europe. She had also been concerned about the Mennonite boys who, though exempt from military conscription, lived and worked as conscientious objectors in camps far from home. Often these young men, several of whom were friends and relatives, were sneered at for not fighting or were accused of being yellow. Of course, this was very hard for them, as it would have been for any young males. So she grieved for them and prayed that they might receive strength to keep the faith.

Keeping the faith and passing it on were very important to both my parents. They felt themselves to be direct inheritors of a spiritual tradition reaching back from the sixteenth-century Mennonite martyrs, thousands of whom died during the Protestant Reformation, to first generation Christians such as Grandmother Lois and Mother Eunice mentioned by the apostle Paul, and even before that to the first disciples of Jesus, who roamed the hills and fields and seas of Galilee.

This spiritual responsibility was a weighty one. So throughout their lives my parents diligently taught us the sacred writings not only by example but also by telling us these stories in daily devotions and by offering spontaneous prayers in which each of us was mentioned by name. Of course, the church, around which community life revolved, reinforced these teachings at Sunday morning worship, funerals, weddings, and baptisms, all of which marked the significant passages of individual lives within the village.

Not surprisingly, an early spiritual experience happened during a Sunday morning worship service when I was four or five years old. I was kneeling beside my mother on the women's side of the sanctuary when somehow her nearness, the warmth of the sun streaming through the high, simple windows, and the comforting drone of the *altesta's* (bishop's) kindly voice as he moved slowly through the cadences of a High German prayer filled me with a spirit of worship. At that moment, I was fully at peace and at home in a world where the physical, emotional, and spiritual aspects of life all flowed together.

Then there is the memory of my fifth birthday. My maternal grandmother, who was dying of stomach and liver cancer, gave me a gift I will never forget. She was a woman who, like my mother, prayed daily with a shawl over her head for all her children and grandchildren, a woman who seemed to be gentle and kind and loving always. I have immortalized her gift to me in a letter:

> *Grandmother, once again, I imagine the day of your dying....The main room (or grotte Schtov, as we used to call it) of the old farmhouse is darkening gradually. The long shadows move slowly but steadily out of the high-ceilinged corners above the metal-framed bed on which you lie, threatening to crowd out the pale autumn light that filters through the narrow space between the partially drawn curtains of the single, long window.*
>
> *But surprisingly, the meagre light persists, struggling against the approaching darkness throughout the long hours of the afternoon.*
>
> *On the bed, surrounded by your grieving sons and daughters, you lie motionless, hands crossed on your stomach, the contours of your body hardly lifting the sheet. Grey hair, usually caught in a braided bun, now fans outwards on a white pillow, while your thin face catches and reflects the light and shadow of the*

*room: dark hollows around the eyes, raised glow of a
brow, jutting nose, and sharp jaw.*

*All is quiet in the room. Only an occasional sniffle
or whisper from one of the watchers as the door opens
and another relative enters to join the vigil.*

*Then suddenly, you speak. A mere trickle of sound,
but enough to prod the watchers into action. They
hurry towards the head of your bed, bend over to
catch your words. But you lift your frail hand and
wave them away.*

*"Maarie," you say. "I want Maarie." Your voice
grows stronger.*

*A woman rises from a high-backed chair near the
window, her swollen body outlined briefly in the
fading light. Heavily she moves towards the bed,
reaches out to touch your hand.*

*"Maarie," you say again, glancing at her body with
a sigh. "So many children already. And doesn't one of
them have a birthday soon? Is it Leona?" Your voice
seems weaker now.*

*"Yes, yes, Leona," my mother says. "But don't you
worry about that. Save your strength. Get better."*

*"No," you say with returning vigour. "She has to
have a present. All children need to be remembered,
especially when there are so many." You raise yourself
slightly as you gesture towards the bedside table. "Give
me that basket. I'll send her a piece of fruit so she'll
know I thought of her on her birthday."*

*My mother, still protesting, hands you the fruit
basket. Your thin pale hand hovers over the oranges,
the apples, the grapes, then touches the only pear.
"That's the one," you say as you pick it up and
carefully place it into my mother's hand. "Give her the
pear. Maybe she's never had one before."*

Your hand falls back on the sheet.

*Later that day when the vigil is over, my weeping
mother returns to our home and somewhere in the
course of her crying remembers to give me that pear.*

*Like you she places the warm, golden fruit carefully
into the palm of my hand and wraps my fingers
around it.*

*Grandmother, forty years after your dying I want to
thank you for that pear. It was the best gift I ever had.
For even as a five-year-old, I knew that to be
remembered by someone on their deathbed made me
special. And being a middle child, I didn't get to feel
special that often; so that pear meant a great deal to
me. Besides, you were right. I'd never had my very
own pear before. It tasted delicious, so soft and so
sweet.*

Looking back on that experience, I don't believe it is coincidental
that my mother now says I'm very much like my grandmother in
mannerisms, character, and quiet expression of faith. Clearly, some
of what the New Testament refers to as the sincere faith of mothers
and grandmothers that first lived in her was passed on to me
when my grandmother gave me that gift of love before she died.
It seems to me now as though part of her body and her being
became part of my body and my being as I ate that delicious fruit.

*And now faith, hope, and love abide, and the greatest
of these is love.*

I Corinthians 13:13

Leona Dueck Penner
Winnipeg, Manitoba

Mennonites, named after Dutch Anabaptist, Menno Simons,
(d.1561), have their roots in the Protestant Reformation. Distinctive
elements of the faith include adult believers' baptism, a simple life
of discipleship based on Christ's teachings of peace and love,
pacifism, and the separation of church and state. The latter two
beliefs led to persecution, martyrdom, and subsequent flight from
country to country in search of a place where adherents would be
free to live their faith.

Mennonites of Swiss–German origin first arrived in North America in the early 1700s; Dutch–Germans followed by way of Russia in the late 1800s and again after each world war. There are approximately 120,000 baptized Mennonites of diverse origins throughout Canada, mostly in Ontario, Manitoba, and British Columbia. Except for Old Order and Amish peoples in southern Ontario and a few small groups in which women still wear a prayer covering, Mennonites are not visibly distinguishable from the rest of Canadian society.

In the past Canadian Mennonites were largely a rural people, known for their strong farming skills. Now increasingly urban, Mennonites are active in human service professions, in business, in politics, and in the arts, especially music. Mennonites are also recognized for their volunteerism and for peace and justice initiatives in Canada and abroad.

THE TRAGEDY OF KARBALA

In the history of Islam no human drama is as compelling in its high tragedy as the story of Karbala. No doubt there are other tragic stories in Islamic history, but the power of the story of Karbala over my mind lies not in its historical but in its archetypal, timeless character, bound by strong emotional ties to what is most sacred in Shia Islam.

Imagine a child of three or four repeatedly exposed to the sacred narrative of Karbala, recounted with dramatic symbolism and expressions of communal sorrow. That is how, as children, my sisters and I first encountered the story. My father was a western-educated, open-hearted Shia Muslim of India. I grew up among people of all religions who were constantly coming to our home. The evenings of every Muharram (first month of the Muslim lunar year) in our home were devoted to the commemoration of the tragedy of Karbala through poetic recitation of the narrative in mournful chants and laments. The atmosphere was replete with sorrow and weeping and occasional rhythmic, ritual beating of the chest, a symbol of shared suffering with the martyrs of Karbala and an affirmation of devotion to and solidarity with the prophet Husain and his family, who sacrificed their lives for faith. The act of weeping was seen as salvific, the sorrow a bond between the mourners and the sacred ones who were mourned.

The seeds of this tragedy go back to the rise of Islam in early seventh century Arabia, with the prophet Muhammad proclaiming a new message: the unity of God and equality of humankind—yes, not merely mankind. This message was so revolutionary that it threatened not only the polytheistic beliefs of innumerable warring tribes but also the social, economic, and gender power structures of the day. That threat gave rise to hostilities against the prophet and his family, particularly in the clan of Banu Ummayya, with Abu Sufyan at its head. The hostilities continued generation after generation, despite the fact that all had embraced Islam. With the spread of Islam from Persia to Syria, wealth flooded the Muslim world, giving rise to luxury and decadence. In 680 CE Yazid, grandson of Abu Sufyan, assumed power in Damascus as the caliph of Muslims and pitted himself against Husain, the saintly grandson of the prophet. So began the great tragedy of Karbala.

As children we knew nothing of this historical backdrop. All we knew was the story as it unfolded with symbolic ceremonies, in deep reverence and sorrow. Here is how that story was recounted:

Yazid, the cruel and depraved caliph in Damascus, demanded that Husain pledge unquestioned allegiance to him as the spiritual head of all Muslims. Yazid knew that unless he had the allegiance of the prophet's family, his oppressive rule could be challenged and he could be overthrown. So he made all attempts to extract allegiance from Husain. But Husain refused. He would not compromise with Yazid's tyrannical rule and thereby disgrace Islam, which championed the oppressed and had always stood for a life of simplicity and austerity. Consequently, Husain's life in Medina was made impossible, and he was hunted from city to city. Then a party in Kufa, Iraq, invited Husain to live among them as their teacher and guide. He accepted the invitation and embarked on the fateful journey to Kufa.

Wide-eyed we listened to the narrator reciting tearfully how Husain left Medina with his family and companions, knowing that he would never return. With a caravan of one hundred men, women, and children, Husain crossed 900 miles (1440 km) of desert on horses and camels, in the scorching Arabian heat.

When he was within a few miles of Kufa, Husain met people coming from Kufa and heard of the terrible murder of his cousin, Ibn Muslim, sent in advance to announce Husain's arrival. Among the men who bore this news was a poet who told Husain not to go on to Kufa, "For the heart of the city is with thee, but its sword is with thine enemies, and the issue rests with God." As Husain was mourning the death of his cousin, a small force of Yazid's army appeared, demanding that he surrender and pledge allegiance to the caliph or face certain death. What a terrible choice! It would mean not only Husain's own death but also the death and suffering of his family and companions. Yet Husain refused once again and so was surrounded by the enemy troops. All routes of escape were blocked. So on the first day of the month of Moharram, Husain camped at Karbala.

The description of Karbala always frightened me—a parched and desolate land with searing heat, howling wind, blowing dust, and this small caravan of anxious men and women, caught in the midst of evil forces, resigned to the will of their God.

For ten days messages passed back and forth between Kufa and Karbala without resolution. The governor of Kufa, under instruction from Damascus, refused all alternatives except a battle. My heart pounded each time I heard that more and more enemy troops arrived at Karbala. They camped at a distance, on the banks of the Euphrates. On the eighth day Husain's access to the water supply was cut off, the abundant streams of the Euphrates still within sight.

The tenth day of Muharram, called Ashura, fell on October 10, 680 CE, and that day Husain's camp was attacked at dawn. It was no battle, seventy men against an army of four thousand, yet Husain's supporters fought valiantly in contempt of death. In horror we heard that his young son, his brother, his very young nephews, and his companions were all brutally massacred. Husain carried the body of each martyr from the massacre field to his camp and laid it on the sand, where his family mourned the death of each loved one. In the end as the sun went down, Husain was alone. He went into the tent to take leave of his family. His sister, Zainab, said that he instructed them to remain firm in their faith, as that was their battle, and that he thanked God for all the blessings bestowed upon him. He then prayed for those who were fighting against him, "not knowing truth from falsehood."

Then Husain took to the battlefield and was immediately surrounded by lancers and swordsmen. After a short while the call for evening prayer was given. Husain got down from his horse and knelt on the sand in prayer. At that moment his head was cut off and raised on a spear as a sign of victory. All Husain's men had already been killed, and the order was given to trample their bodies under the horses' hooves. That night the enemy troops marched into Husain's camp, looted, and then burned the tents. Terrified and grief-stricken, the women, children, and Husain's sick son, Abid, left the burning tents behind to sojourn alone on the burning sand under the night sky.

Husain's family was then taken captive—Abid in chains, holding the rope of a camel; the severed head of Husain in front, paraded on a spear. Under army escort, the family was taken to Kufa and then Damascus. No one knew who they were or what had happened. The story of Karbala would have been lost were it not for Husain's sister, Zainab, who recounted the tragedy wherever the caravan stopped, soldiers whipping her each time she spoke. And so the story of Karbala was preserved.

To me the story was about the faith and suffering and martyrdom of the most sacred and holy beings in my religious tradition: the beloved family members of the holy prophet, caught in the terrors of history as they stood against the world for the sake of truth and justice. Husain died a martyr, bearing witness, and that witness redeemed what would otherwise be known as a failure and defeat. His martyrdom dealt a death blow to the corrupt regime at Damascus and all it stood for.

I grew up listening to this narrative over and over again, chanted lyrically in my mother tongue, Urdu, a beautiful language born of a blending of classical Sanskrit, Persian, and Arabic. The narrative evoked powerful images: images of massacre and desperation; of courage, pain, and pathos; of love and faith and sacrifice; images of captive women, wounded at heart by the horrors of the day, wandering through the desolate desert night; images of burning tents and enemy soldiers encroaching with burning torches. At eight years of age in the early hours of the morning of Ashura, suddenly, I too was at Karbala, sobbing on the sand, terrified, helpless, sick at heart with the burden of grief and rage. My mother could hardly control me as I fell to pieces.

Out of the shock and pain at the sudden experience of the inexorable betrayal of all I held sacred, my heart broke open, and gradually, without my realizing it, my emotional and spiritual response was no longer confined to the suffering of Husain and his family but extended to every incident of brutality and injustice, wherever it occurred. Later through stories and poetry in Urdu I learned also about the crucifixion of Jesus Christ. Slowly my understanding also grew about Jesus' suffering willingly, remaining loyal to his message, refusing to render evil for evil. And again I found myself facing the same spiritual anguish as when I thought of Karbala. These two events in the religious history of humankind have affected me so profoundly that I dare not think about them too deeply or too realistically. If I do, I feel I may crumble again. But deep down each time a tragedy of tyranny and injustice occurs, the story of Karbala awakens and is re-enacted deep within me; each time a new cross is erected in a personal Calvary.

Pondering all these things, I have gradually moved to the conviction that God resides not in prayer and fasting alone but more so in faithfulness to one's truth and in the willingness to fight against wrong until death, in love and pain and suffering, through the eternal battle between good and evil.

Zohra Husaini
Edmonton, Alberta

Distinctions between Sunnis and Shi'ites—the two major groups in the Muslim world—revolve primarily around religious authority and succession. Shi'ites believe succession continued through Muhammad's own family, beginning with his son-in-law, Ali. Ali, however, was assassinated in 661, as was his son, Husain, in 680 at Karbala. Mu'awiyah retained power as caliph but lost support from those who contested his right to succeed.

Shi'ites also regard Ali as the first imam, which is why the question of ongoing religious authority is closely aligned with that of succession. In Shia Islam imams are the rightful leaders in both spiritual and temporal domains. Among Sunni Muslims imams are cast in a more pragmatic, less mystical, role as leaders of local congregations. Rather than look to imams as invested with divine authority, Sunnis regard the Qur'an and its interpretation by the *sunna* (tradition) as the true authoritative basis of Islam.

The loss of rightful successors through the massacre at Karbala, Iraq, is central to Shi'ism: Karbala is not only a critical historical event but a living paradigm for suffering and the resistance of evil. The victimization of Husain, his family, and his companions is commemorated in passion plays and mournful processions. The annual observance of their martyrdom, on 10 Muharram (the first month of the Islamic year), is the single most powerful religious event for Shia Muslims.

Iran and parts of Iraq are home to a majority of Shi'ites; sizeable communities also exist in India. Shi'ites in Canada are concentrated largely in metropolitan centres.

POINTING TO THE HEART:
Interreligious Dialogue in Montreal

It had not been long since my superior had called me into his office to say he wanted me to work full-time in interreligious dialogue. I had suggested we prepare an interfaith prayer for peace, modelled after the one done in Assisi, in October of 1986.

After many phone calls, I was finally seated on the floor of a Buddhist temple, awaiting the venerable monk who was in charge, with the intention of inviting him to take part in the event. It was not the first time I had sat in a Buddhist temple, but then I had been in India doing personal research. This time I was here to beg, in all humility, that the prayer leader come and share with us his prayers for peace.

It was a difficult meeting in one way because the monk spoke neither French nor English, but through gestures, photographs, and so on we managed to communicate, and I promised to come back. Just as I was about to leave, someone came in, and the monk asked this person to convey regrets about the language barrier. I looked at the monk. "It's all right," I said, pointing to my chest. "The heart understands." He smiled. Months later I met the same monk again. Someone was about to introduce us when the monk looked at me with a smile and pointed to his heart. This for me was living proof that the dialogue I was about to undertake had to be rooted in heart values.

Over ten years have passed since then. As I look back, I can only do so with gratitude not only for what has been accomplished here in Montreal but for all that I have received. If I feel so at ease working with people of all faiths, it is simply because this is something which was given as a grace from my early childhood.

As a child brought up in Trinidad, a small cosmopolitan island in the West Indies, my first concept of God came from all that surrounded me. I played in a street where most of my friends were Christian, but the milkmaid who came to our door with a large pail of milk on her head wore a sari and distinctive marks that my mother told me were Hindu. Many a night we fell asleep to the sound of Shango drums coming from the hills. A woman who came to help my mother with the cooking and cleaning belonged to this African religion. I remember she was afraid of thunder because for her it was the voice of God. Then there was the annual Muslim commemoration of the martyrdom of the saint, Husain, and a parade filled with drumming and hymn singing in the streets. And we had only to drive a half-hour out of the city to be among rice fields, Hindu prayer flags, and small temples.

As kids we all got along so well together. When I left Trinidad and came to live in Montreal, I lost not only my friends but also the religious variety which had surrounded me as a child. At the time the main religions in the city were Christianity and Judaism. Of course, because of my early entry into monastic life—just one year after arriving in Montreal—I was steeped in Catholicism.

Over the last twenty-odd years, the city's religious landscape has changed completely. Now there are over thirty Buddhist centres, some of which are pagodas, several Hindu and Sikh temples, and also Muslim mosques. Montreal is one of the most beautiful cities (if not the most beautiful city) in North America. An island sitting in the St. Lawerence River, Montreal has perhaps the most bicycle trails of any major city and in summer becomes one long festival of celebrations. People from almost every country in the world live here, and there are languages, foods, and customs from every culture.

The first real work in the field of interreligious dialogue in Montreal was started some thirty years ago at what was known as the Monchanin Centre, with Jacques Langlais, Robert Vachon, and Kalpana Dass. It was there that I was first able to assist at a concert of sacred music of India and with conferences given by people involved in interfaith activities. Men such as Raimondo Pannikar and Dom Tholens left profound impressions on me.

My first visit to India in 1971 and a full sabbatical year in 1981 were attempts to train myself to work in this field. Being officially nominated by our Franciscan superior in 1987 was just a confirmation of the work I already had so much at heart. When we started the interfaith peace prayer in Montreal, the event was to be a means for different religious leaders in the city to come together. My dream was that once we met and got to know and respect one another, prejudices would disappear, and we would be able to work together, finally, for survival.

I see part of this dream becoming a reality. Some people have become friends through all these years; others have passed on. I think sometimes of the Tibetan Buddhist monk who encouraged me in this work and who died during his meditation. I went to the temple for the funeral and was taken into his room to see him before the funeral rites. He was seated on his bed in the same posture as when he had died three days before, and his body was still intact. I remember his telling me that we were brothers—and to think that he passed away on the feast of St. Francis.

St. Francis is a great source of inspiration to me. Francis of Assisi lived during the crusades, at a time when Christians denounced the Muslim invaders, and a terrible battle raged between the two religions. At a moment of truce in 1219 in Damietta, Egypt, near the River Nile—only 250 miles (400 km) from where American troops were stationed during the Gulf war—Francis took a companion and crossed the lines to speak directly to the sultan,

Malik al-Kamel. The story tells how these two men went on to become friends. Later on Francis wrote for friars who wished to live among Muslims, instructing the brothers to do so in a spirit of humility.

It is in this same spirit of humility and service that I also wish to do interfaith work.

Yet one of the challenges religion faces today is not only how we get along but how we transmit our spiritual values to youth so that they find value in life itself. I often travel on the subway, and when I do, I become aware of the new society being formed. I look at the young generation and realize how, despite their parents' cultural or religious backgrounds, youngsters are so similar in the way they dress, the music they listen to, and the films and games they share. Spiritual values are being forsaken or, more so, not being absorbed. Suicide rates in Quebec are among the highest in the world and so prevalent among kids. How can they come to see that we must have a thirst for the knowledge of others, ourselves, and the mysteries of life? How can the youth come to see that we find value in life when we love and that love leads us to serve? For if young people are not receiving these basic spiritual values on which religion is founded, how can our religious traditions ever survive?

Since the first interfaith peace prayer in Montreal, many links of friendship have been created over the years among Christians, Jews, Buddhists, Hindus, Native peoples, Baha'is, and many others. Now I wonder if it might be time to begin working on another level. How can we help one another to face challenges in the world today? How can we transmit values in a language which speaks to youth? Are we to leave it up to Hollywood to portray goodness in star warriors who struggle to overcome evil? Or to pop musicians to imagine "What if God was one of us?"

Computer experts have now made a toy that needs to be cared for or it will expire. One kid told me, "If I don't attend to him, he'll die." Society sells products which appeal to youth's spiritual needs, and marketing has found a means of reaching them. Perhaps we have something to learn here. It is my conviction that unless we can sit together peacefully and consider these facts, we will remain at the beginning of a long journey.

Still, there is yet hope, for our God is one of hope, and in many an aged body there is a spirit of eternal youth ready to help and renew those who are willing to serve.

Rolph Fernandes
Montreal, Quebec

Love of devoted service to others is but one aspect of the centuries-old attraction to the Franciscan way of life. Simplicity, humility, poverty, and prayer are the foundations of the order, founded by one of Christendom's most popular saints, Francis of Assisi (d. 1226).

Franciscans have been a spiritual force in Canadian religious history for almost four hundred years. Along with the Jesuits, Franciscans were part of France's missionizing efforts among Indigenous peoples; the first Franciscans were Recollet priests who arrived in New France in 1615. Other Franciscan orders soon followed: Friars Minor, Conventuals, Capuchins, and the cloistered women's order known as Poor Clares. Franciscans rapidly established themselves as educators, with schools in Trois Rivières, Longueil, and Sorel, as Quebec grew into a Catholic stronghold and the model of triumphalism in North America.

The Quiet Revolution, however, changed all that. The Catholic Church, which had dominated public institutions, suffered deep losses among both lay and religious, as Quebec plunged headlong into reforms that changed the face of the province and the future of the nation. In the 1960s there were six hundred Franciscans distributed throughout eastern Canada and in three New England states; now there are fewer than 120. (Worldwide there are about forty thousand Franciscans and Poor Clares.) As the number of novices dropped, the average age of religious rose as well.

Franciscans, however, remain positive despite such statistics. Today, the order is confronting an uncertain future by re-envisioning its mission and deepening commitments to the poor and disenfranchised. Following in their founder's footsteps, Franciscans continue to support interfaith dialogue and peace activism in Canada and throughout the world.

THE DONKEY
AND THE JACKAL

Storytelling has been the pedagogical fountainhead of Hinduism throughout the ages. Nowhere, perhaps, is this narrative tradition more deeply rooted than in India, where this art form is still the most popular medium of transmitting the spirit of her cultural heritage. Even here in Canada this tradition continues, as Hindus delight in listening to the same stories that entertained their ancestors age after age.

Stories ingeniously woven into mythologies, epics, and fables focus on the nature of human behaviour. From the sublime heights of religion and philosophy to the ridiculous intrigues and deceits of animals in fables, these stories give voice to human triumphs and foibles, and they form the tapestry of Hindu storytelling tradition. Episodes that relate the origins and functions of gods and goddesses, their heroic exploits, and the misdeeds of miscreant animals personifying human behaviour never fail to amuse and give pleasure to the Hindu listener.

Morals aside, the capacity of such stories to entertain excites the imaginative fantasy of many a youngster. This was no less true of me when I was a boy growing up in rural Trinidad. I was fascinated by these stories and never lost an opportunity to attend occasions at which they were told. Their profound impact has instilled in me an introspective nature that enables me to comprehend the world of human behaviour with sensitivity. Nowhere have I found this experience more useful than in the classroom. As a teacher at both the elementary and secondary school levels I found storytelling to be a remarkable tool. Employed as an illustrative technique, it simplified abstract ideas and concepts in literature and unravelled complex life situations. The unbelievable power of the story worked magic, animating listless students and stimulating unmotivated ones. Emotionally, storytelling not only drew me closer to my students, it allowed me to re-enter the world of my childhood. That power resonates with the magic of my early days, as you will now discover.

One peripatetic storyteller, sporting a long beard, especially charmed me with his contagious laugh and syrupy voice. Seated in a lotus position, he expounded his stuff to eager audiences. He had the aura of an ancient, wise monk, and he possessed a phenomenal memory. Without books or notes he spun his nightly yarns, drawing freely from Hindu epics and fables. Like a playful animal enjoying his theatrics, the storyteller had the gift of weaving story after story into a whole without losing the main idea of each episode. To this day two stories in particular still delight me. One is about a donkey, and it goes like this:

On festival days the temple priest would place a statue of the celebrated deity on the back of a donkey. The temple keeper would then drive the donkey through the city streets for all to honour the god or goddess. Being very pious, the people made colouful garlands and worshipped the images. The devotees also offered oblations of water and milk to the idols and as a show of gratitude to the donkey, caressed and patted it, whispering sweet words into his ears.

Overwhelmed by this demonstration of religious fervour, the donkey felt that he too was being worshipped. He became very proud, basking in the vainglory of his importance. "What special karmas I have!" he said to himself. "I am blessed to have humans worship me. These humans think that they are the only smart ones and that my kind are stupid and stubborn. This is my chance to prove to them how dependent they are on me."

Then one sunny day as thousands lined the streets on the birthday festival of Ganesh, the elephant-headed god and remover of obstacles, the headstrong donkey refused to move. He sat down, head slumped firmly on the ground. As much as the temple keeper tried to push the donkey along, the man could not make the obstinate animal budge. Curious, the children stood by and watched. Amused by this struggle between man and animal, they laughed at and mocked the donkey. Adults waiting to pay obeisance to the deity grew impatient at this display of bestial defiance. But the donkey, master of the situation, was enjoying his victory. "I will make these callous humans sweat," he muttered to himself.

The angry keeper, frustrated and embarrassed by his inability to shake the animal, whacked it with a big stick that he carried expressly for this purpose. At long last the donkey jumped up in pain. To the horror of the devotees, the idol of Ganesh came crashing to the ground, shattering into pieces. The donkey, true to his nature, hee-hawing at the blows as if he were being murdered, bolted through the streets, sending the crowd into a frenzied stampede. And what was intended as a grand celebration turned out to be a spectacle of a contest between man and animal, ending in sheer pandemonium and chaos.

At this point in the stillness of the tropical night, the storyteller would pause for dramatic effect, take a sip of water, and chuckle to himself, pleased with the expressions of happiness in his captive audience. And the listeners, forgetting the hardships of the day gone by and unmindful of the new day to come, sat enjoying every bit of the drama. The children, half-sleepy, not anxious to see the end of a good night, would plead and ask to be treated to one more story.

The old bard would then smilingly caress his long beard. "This is the last one I am going to tell tonight," he said. "It is a wonderful story. I learned it from my mother, whose grandmother taught it in India."

Soon the ancient tale came to life before our eyes.

Once in the forest there lived an old jackal. Being a slow hunter and unable to fight for his share of the kill, he could never quite get enough to eat. One day he wandered into a neighbouring city in search of food. Some fierce city dogs saw the intruder and barking furiously, gave chase. Confused and frightened, the jackal ran helter-skelter for cover. Ultimately, he stumbled into the backyard of a dye-maker, where a vat of indigo stood under an open shed. Up jumped the desperate jackal into the vat, and in the nick of time, for soon the pack of mad hounds were on the spot. Not seeing the jackal and losing track of his smell, the dogs left frustrated, yelping their disappointment.

Quietly the jackal emerged and shrank away into the forest. The other animals could not believe what they saw. They were amazed at this strange creature. "What is this blue animal we see?" they asked one another. "We have not seen one like this before. Incredible! He must have been sent by the King of the Heavens to rule over us." The rascal, of course, heard them and seized the opportunity. With majestic grace he mounted a rock and addressed them all.

"Oh my dear friends, give me your ears! How sensible you are! You are quite right. I have, indeed, been sent by my father above, King of Heaven, to rule over you. Therefore, obey me now and do my bidding. Those who prove themselves to be loyal subjects will be promoted to higher positions, but those who disobey will be banished forever."

This speech left no doubt as to who was in charge. The jackal spoke with such great authority and conviction, even his arch enemies believed him and admired his royal armour.

And so the old jackal became king. Everyone swore allegiance to him. He made the lion prime minister; the tiger, lord-in-waiting; the elephant, the door keeper; the monkey, valet, and so on. But the new king had his fellow jackals beaten and driven away. Undaunted, his own cousins hunted him and laid in wait to settle old scores.

And so for a while the blue jackal lived in glory, enjoying the pomp and ceremony that befits a king. Then one fateful day he heard the yowls of a pack of jackals in the distance. This was music to his ears. Thrilled by the sound and overcome with joy, instinctively he returned the howl, forgetting in that split second his disguise as king.

No sooner had he cried out than the lion and tiger and all the other animals detected the deceit of the phoney king. Infuriated that they had been made to look like a pack of fools serving a lowly jackal, the animals cornered him. Circled by this horde of sworn enemies, the poor old jackal could not escape their bloody fury. And so ended the short-lived reign of the pretender.

On this didactic note the night of stories concluded; we would have to wait until another visit from the sage storyteller.

The poignancy of these stories has left me with impressions that resonate to this day. My formative years in values-building were nurtured by such fables. Like oases in a desert they sometimes nourished the arid and tedious moments in my life. How often the sad mockery of life would be lightened with these spirited, sophisticated animal metaphors.

The character of the donkey lingers on as a constant reminder of how a false ego proves doubly destructive when accompanied by asinine attitudes and the necessity to guard against a narcissistic nature lest we suffer a proverbial whipping. The blue jackal, a colourful caricature, forces us to confront the evils of insulting the intelligence of others, not to mention the consequences of pretending to be what we are not.

Both the donkey and the jackal subtly nudge us to view the world anew—not with blinded eyes but with the innocence of a child and the mind of a sincere seeker.

Deo Kernahan
Etobicoke, Ontario

Unlike Christianity, Buddhism, and Islam, all of which trace their origins to a particular founder, Hinduism is not attributable to any one figure. The roots of the world's most complex religion reach back almost six thousand years to the Indus Valley civilization. Hinduism, however, cannot be reduced to a unified system that stems from a single source.

The philosophy of Hinduism is grounded in the principles of eternal truths (*sanatan*) that govern the cosmos and right conduct (dharma) in human affairs. These truths, which have been intuited by sages over the centuries, appear in a multitude of scriptures and animate the vast array of stories in Hindu mythology.

As a way of life Hinduism represents respect for all other ways of life: monotheism, monism, polytheism, agnosticism, and atheism are all included in the diverse paths of Hinduism. Hindus do, however, believe in only one God—the unmanifested, imperishable Brahma, who is beyond description and qualities. All creation and manifestations are considered sacred; everything from a grain of sand to the greatest star is a divine spark of God's will.

Nearly 80 percent of India's one billion people call themselves Hindus. Of the approximately 750 million Hindus worldwide, about 250,000 live in Canada. The major influx of Hindus has been since 1967, with the largest concentration settling in Ontario. Strong emphasis on family, education, and non-violence enable Hindus to integrate well into Canadian society, while Hindu stories, temples, festivals, ritual observances, sacred music, and dance enrich the nation's wealth of cultural resources.

DANNY'S TOY TRUCK

After his enlightenment experience at the age of thirty-five, the
Buddha spent the next forty-five years wandering about the
northeast corner of India, teaching interested people in whatever
town or village he came to, much the same way as Socrates did.

One day, the Buddha was walking along on his way to one
more destination, another day of teaching the dharma, when a
young man stopped him to ask, "Sir, I couldn't help but notice
that you seem so serene, you seem to radiate goodness and
wisdom. Are you a god?"

"Most definitely not," replied the Buddha.

"Well, are you an angel, then?"

"I don't think so."

"Then you're a saint."

"I wouldn't describe myself that way."

"Are you a man then?" The young man began to get exasperated.

"No, I'm not a man, either."

"Then what are you, sir?"

"I am awake."

My first religious experience, such as it was, took place when I was about six years old. Our grade one class was being marched to the cathedral in Saint John, New Brunswick, for our first confession, in preparation for our first Holy Communion. I remember it was a sunny day, and as we approached the cathedral, I had a feeling of dread. Even at that age churches inspired fear in me.

We cued up in two long lines on either side of Father C.'s confessional. The lines moved gradually but steadily until it was my turn. I entered the confessional, knelt down, and waited for the priest to open the compartment. Everything was sombre and dark, and I was very nervous.

Then the compartment slid open, and I could see the vague outline of a man's head through the little holes in the grill.

Feeling somewhat overwhelmed, I stayed silent. "Yes, my son?" Father C. asked. I then recited what the teacher had taught us to say, "Bless me Father, for I have sinned. I confess to Almighty God and to you, Father. This is my first confession." I fell silent, and again the priest had to prompt me to continue.

I stammered that I didn't have any sins. "But that's impossible, my son, we all have sins," he explained. "You must remember something you have done. Have you spoken out against either your father or mother?" No. He then recited a list of possible transgressions, and to each of these I replied no. This was definitely not what I had expected, and time began to take on a strangely eternal quality. Father C. was growing impatient, yet even after racking my brain, I could find nothing that would warrant confessing. But I was not to get off easily. The priest insisted there was some sin I was simply not remembering.

At this point my awareness expanded to take in the entire situation—here I was in the confessional with all my friends waiting outside, and as near as I could figure, I had already been in here a long time. It became clear to me that Father C. wasn't going to let me leave unless I came up with something.

"I stole my friend Danny Losier's toy truck," I blurted out.

"Ah ha, you see! I knew there was a sin in there somewhere," the priest thundered. "Well listen here, young man, I want you to come back to my confessional next Friday to tell me that you've returned the toy truck to that boy." And he shut the small compartment with a thud. I was sweating bullets by this time, I was so nervous. But not so nervous that I didn't realize he hadn't given me absolution! That didn't seem quite so bad, since I hadn't really stolen the truck. On the other hand, I had just lied to get out of the confessional.

As he requested, I returned the following Friday to tell another lie, that I had returned Danny Losier's toy truck. Father C. then gave me absolution and Hail Marys as penance. I left the confessional feeling much better than the first time but perplexed. The fallout from this intense experience was to linger for many years.

In the summer of 1970, the day after I completed my last undergraduate course at the University of New Brunswick, a friend and I took the bus to Saint John to visit my parents. I wasn't sure at the time, but it was to say goodbye. We stayed overnight in the overcrowded Cormier household, and the next day we took the train to Montreal. I had a small vinyl suitcase and 50 dollars in my pocket. That was it.

Leaving home wasn't difficult because I had no idea what I would do if I stayed. A phase of my life had ended; it was time to move on. I didn't intend to stay in Montreal long, however, since I'd been accepted into graduate studies at the University of British Columbia. When I arrived in Montreal, I first stayed with wonderful friends who treated me like family and helped me get my first job. I spent the summer getting to know the city, making new friends, and writing poetry. One day I remembered that my friend and mentor, Alden Nowlan, had given me the number of one T. Donnern and suggested that I look him up.

I visited Donnern in his newly rented mansion, where he was setting up a meditation centre, having been authorized to do so by a monk. Or so he said. Who was I to argue? We talked about poetry and other subjects, and Donnern was critical of just about everything. He also had a tendency to talk for long periods without pausing for a breath. (Thinking back on it now, that should have been a warning.) I didn't have a clue about Buddhism, so I didn't say much, but I did say that I didn't like religion, that I thought it existed to control and exploit people. I didn't see why Buddhism should be an exception.

It was when I was finally tired and getting ready to leave that he asked if I'd like to see the meditation room. He had set up the room very well. There was a carved wooden Buddha at the north end of the room, bathed in golden light from a lamp on the mantelpiece. Small square mats were lined up facing each wall. Round, brown meditation cushions filled with kapok sat on each mat. The atmosphere was peaceful.

Donnern asked if I'd like to meditate with him for a few minutes. Being a curious, what-the-hell kind of person, I agreed. He gave me some basic instructions, and I sat down. I had no idea how to sit properly, so I sat cross-legged, hands in my lap. I concentrated on breathing, being aware of each in-breath and out-breath. It seemed like only seconds when he tinkled some bell and the meditation was over.

I rose from the cushion surprisingly refreshed and energized. I figured meditation might be something to try out on a regular basis. Donnern must have read my mind. He said he was renting out rooms for 25 dollars a month. I told him I'd think it over.

I never did make it to B.C., and by September I began to feel as if I were wearing out my welcome with friends. So once again I thought, what the hay. I called up Donnern and said I'd rent a room from him. I moved in September 26th; by the time I moved out, December 28th, four years later, it seemed as if an eternity had passed. I'd been on an odyssey, and I wasn't the only one. Donnern's marriage had collapsed from abuse, and he'd taken in several women students who, years later, would describe to me the conditions which they and their children (by Donnern) had endured. The hoped-for spiritual haven had turned into a prison.

In retrospect, I wonder why I put up with it all. It wasn't until after I left the centre and began to research his background (something I recommend be done ahead of time and not after the fact!) that I realized the full extent of the abuse. But I had really wanted to learn how to meditate. Sure it was hard. We awoke each day at 5:30 for 6 AM meditation. There was pain in the knees, the butt, the ankles, neck, and shoulders; we had to be alert or Donnern would knock us off our cushions. But I took to meditation like a fish to water and was determined to learn all I could.

Why did I take so readily to meditation? One day when I was three years old, my uncles were in the field near my Grandpa's house threshing hay. It was a beautiful blue-sky day, and they took me with them (Uncle Dosith was my favourite because he laughed a lot) and sat me on a big grey rock in the middle of the field. And as they worked, I watched with great intensity the movement of the hand-held scythes and the falling sheaves of golden hay, following the rhythm of each movement with my eyes. Then as I was concentrating, each shaft of hay took on a life of its own as it was cut and felled like a huge tree, crashing to the ground below. There I was, just sitting on that great round rock in the middle of the field, watching my uncles threshing hay. But it was as though in that moment my mind opened a little to take in more of what was really there.

That moment of great mental clarity stayed in my memory, and I recalled it when I first learned to meditate.

Eventually, during the four years I lived at the centre, I read books on Buddhism and met with teachers such as Piyadassi Mahathera from Sri Lanka, Hsuan Hua Shih from the Chinese Ch'an tradition, and Kalu Rinpoche from the Tibetan Kagyu tradition. It was with the latter that I "took refuge" in the summer of 1971 in Magog, Quebec, meaning I adopted the teachings of Buddha as my spiritual path. These were great teachers from whom I learned a lot and who helped me get out of a now dire situation.

In the dead of night near the end of 1974, I fled the centre. Finally, I was free to take up the serious study and practice of Tibetan Buddhism and I did so with the lama who was to become my teacher until his death in 1994. This was Geshe Khenrab Gajam, who had been sent to Montreal to serve the Tibetan community.

What have I learned these many years? Not nearly enough: no matter how difficult life gets, no matter what the setbacks, keep slogging. Spiritual progress is sometimes like swimming through concrete, so be patient. And spiritual practice isn't so much like a business deal; it's more like mountain climbing, foolish but exhilarating. Besides, as time flows on, you might get to know one particular individual better and better. Yourself.

Oh, and one other thing. In spiritual life, as in everything else, don't take no wooden nickels.

Louis Cormier
LaSalle, Quebec

Indian Buddhism first made its way to Tibet around the late eighth century and included both Hindu yogic and tantric practices, along with the classical teachings of the historical Buddha (500 BCE). At that time two paths to enlightenment were acknowledged. Sutra (sacred text) practice was based on morality, concentration, and wisdom (perceiving reality free from social and psychic conditioning). The other path, which became the cornerstone of the Tibetan traditions, was tantric, a practice which blended the sutra teachings with techniques adapted from Hindu systems of yoga and tantra.

The aim of tantric systems is to transform the basic human passions of desire and aversion, for the purpose of spiritual development. Rather than denying such primal urges, tantra purifies them into wholesome and helpful forces. Skill in both self-control and acceptance are necessary to be successful with tantric work. Buddhist Tantrism is also known as Vajrayana.

Vajrayana incorporates the major aspects of both the Theravada and Mahayana Buddhist teachings and is basically an esoteric extension of them. The Tibetan tantric path includes the *Lamrim* (stages of the path), indispensable topics for reflection and contemplation, and the meditations and activities that follow. The *Lamrim* embodies the necessary prerequisites for tantra and is set out as a progressive set of steps. These include: relying upon a spiritual guide (learning from someone already on the path); recognizing the preciousness of human life (the importance of using life for something valuable); accepting the inevitability of death and impermanence; taking refuge from *samsara*—the cycle of endless grasping and eventual disappointment; understanding karma (the law of cause and effect); remembering the kindness of others; equalizing self and others (realizing that we all want to be happy); understanding the disadvantage of self-cherishing; knowing the advantage of cherishing others; developing compassion; taking responsibility for relieving others' burdens; sharing one's good fortune with others; *bodhichitta* (the desire to attain full enlightenment for the sake of all beings); tranquil abiding (developing advanced stages of concentration); and superior seeing (developing emptiness—that is recognizing the non-fixed nature of one's personal ego).

China's ongoing occupation of Tibet means that some 150,000 Tibetans remain in exile in India and elsewhere, including Canada. These are guided by the fourteenth Dalai Lama, who was awarded the Nobel Peace Prize for his efforts to preserve Tibetan culture in diaspora. In North America glamorous film depictions of Tibetan Buddhism obscure the fact that as with all great Buddhist traditions, the practice requires a great deal of commitment and hard work. There is no concept of a creator god or saviour; the onus is on the individual to see the good sense of spiritual practice and to persist for the benefit of all.

CHILDREN OF THE GODS

In the dreamtime long ago before the beginning of all things the goddess floated in the abyss of the outer darkness, alone. All the love and joy, all the pain and sorrow that ever were and ever could be, she contained within herself. As there was naught to whom she could express herself, she gazed upon the sea of her own being and dreamed the sky of another who was at once herself and yet other. Out of love and in great suffering she drew her own heart's desire from within, and the Lord of the Dance of Life was born. She knew at once that she would be all-encompassing space to his everlasting time. He knew at once that she was both his source and his destiny. Out of love he embraced her, and the ecstasy of their mating erupted in an enthusiasm of creation from which the living, singing universe was born.

As members of that living universe, Wiccans understand themselves and all living beings not only as an expression of the gods but as part of them. This understanding is reflected in the common blessings "Thou art God" and "Thou art Goddess," which serve to remind us that as children born of the love of the Goddess and the God, we are not to judge and condemn but to learn and grow in love and compassion. When the time allotted for each mortal passage runs out, and we find ourselves reunited with our divine parents, it is our goal to stand before them naked and unafraid. We shall not be wearing academic gowns or laurel wreaths or medals but the scars we have earned along the way.

I had walked the Wiccan path for decades when it led me beneath the razor-wire arbour surrounding the steel gates of William Head Institution, a medium-security penitentiary for men. In the past I had never felt any particular sympathy for, never mind kinship with, convicted criminals. With little fanfare I was directed to the academic building and found myself walking, unescorted, into the unguarded classroom where I was to teach anthropology to the twenty students enrolled in the Simon Fraser University Prison Education Program. They'd put the run on every other female instructor who had come into the prison, and the gleam in their eyes told me they were determined to do the same to me. Their acid test, however, was easily neutralized. Biting humour was an approach to which they were singularly unaccustomed and to which they were unable to respond defensively. Intimidation tactics may have worked with all the other women in your lives, I thought, as I stared back at them, but they won't work with this one!

At first the men seemed confused; then one by one they shifted their approach. If they couldn't put the run on me, they'd do the chivalrous thing and take care of me instead. Many had entered the program with a belligerent attitude they had adopted to hide their low self-esteem and deep feelings of unworthiness. My delight with their small offerings of home-made cookies seemed to please them. Within days of my arrival they insisted upon escorting me back to the prison gates after each class. We settled into a productive and pleasant working relationship, and they quickly gained a sense of self-mastery and self-confidence. Smiles began to replace scowls as the long-neglected spirit within was rekindled. Their quest for the inner grail—that divine spark at the core of our higher, true selves, which had been only dimly apprehended at first—was pursued with enthusiasm. I too was enjoying the quest, as I realized that teaching at William Head was as much a learning experience for me as it was for my students.

To this day I am grateful for those lessons, many of which were learned in the pastoral surroundings outside the classroom. The prison, affectionately dubbed "Club Fed," is located on a point of land southwest of Victoria. Tall stands of Garry oaks grace sprawling lawns above the rocky shore of the Strait of Juan de Fuca. Deer graze peacefully on the nine-hole golf course, raccoons clamber up the trees, and flocks of Canada geese nest each spring in a protected cove below the visitors' centre.

While I was teaching there, one of the resident fawns lost its mother and was rescued by an inmate. He fed the fawn from a bottle and kept it warm overnight in a corner of the greenhouse. Watching him lavish love on his small charge, we witnessed what was perhaps the first truly caring relationship with another living being he'd ever been able to establish. I watched as well when the guards came to take the fawn away from him. Pets weren't allowed, and the fawn was "shipped." The inmate was heartbroken.

Another prisoner had rescued a pair of baby raccoons from starvation when they were orphaned. I was introduced to them when I'd been granted special permission to tour parts of the grounds normally off limits. The guards knew nothing of the masked bandits. Yet their adoptive parent managed to nurture them to adulthood, by which time they were convinced that they too were human. So human, in fact, that during one of the performances of William Head On Stage (WHOS)—the only inmate theatre in Canada open to the general public—the raccoons invited themselves in. By the time they were discovered, they'd managed to reduce considerably the stock of donuts on the refreshment tables. The guests were delighted; the warden was not.

It was not the first time sharpshooters had been ordered into the prison. The inmates who had befriended the deer, raccoons, and several stray cats stood frozen, horror-stricken, and silent as the rifles were fired and the animals they loved fell around them one by one. I wept with the men not only for this mindless and spiteful carnage but for the inmates themselves, for the pain and loss they had endured witnessing the slaughter of the innocents.

The Canada geese had escaped the firing squad but not the destruction. Guards were sent out to find their nests and reduce the number of geese by shaking all of the eggs in several nests rather than a few in each. Some goslings hatched, but several pairs of geese, mates for life, stood huddled and forlorn beside their doomed eggs. The parents' sorrow, too, was deeply felt by many of the prisoners.

During this period I had come to see each of my students as I saw myself—as a child of the gods, here to learn lessons in a world where there are no limits to what the gods may demand of us. But how far could this feeling of kinship be pushed? I was about to find out.

The staging of most plays requires both male and female actors. In an all-male prison, female actors must be brought in from the outside. Intrigued by my husband's involvement with the prison as a lawyer and mine as a university instructor, our elder daughter, a drama enthusiast, decided to volunteer to act in a WHOS play one autumn. "Be professional! Do not become involved with anyone!" were her father's famous last words of admonition.

The following spring T.M. let her world-transforming intentions be known. "You're going to marry Rick?" I exclaimed. He was one of my students, president of the theatre troupe and the lead actor in the next play. The play had been written by my husband, Gary, and he had agreed to help with the directing. Rick and Gary were going to have to work together on that production. The entire prison held its collective breath.

On August 17, 1993, T.M. and Rick were legally married and handfasted by Wiccan rite in William Head Institution. They now have two beautiful daughters. Rick is on parole and will be the rest of his life; but we treasure him as part of our family and are proud of his determination to return to school to complete his education—an education that was interrupted when the same warden who had suspended the lives of deer, raccoons, and cats decided to suspend the university program as well. Education, like pets, was unacceptable in a system based on retribution rather than restoration and healing.

Now whenever I reflect on my time at William Head or look at my son-in-law, I think about the scars and I'm reminded that whatever challenges we create for ourselves in this life, we are all children of the gods, earth-seed for a short time only before destiny claims us, and once more we take root among the stars

Heather Botting
Victoria, British Columbia

The Wiccan religion has its origins in the aboriginal, earth-based traditions of pre-Christian Europe. Wicca is not concerned with historical figures, founders, or events, but with the mysterious elemental forces manifest in the cycles of the seasons and mirrored in the human psyche. Wiccan spirituality is based on nature-as-scripture and emphasizes the immanence of divinity in both its feminine and masculine manifestations.

The primary symbol of the Wiccan tradition is the sacred marriage of the Goddess and the God, a union from which all creation is understood to have been wrought. As the wheel of the year turns through one complete revolution, Wiccans participate in eight "sabbats," or solar festivals, and numerous "esbats," or lunar rites, to celebrate the mysteries of birth, death, and re-birth associated with the sacred marriage. Participants in solar rites honour the God for his role in serving the Goddess and follow his example in serving her themselves through the lunar rites.

With profound respect for the earth as a manifestation of the Divine, and inspired by the unconditional mutual love between the Goddess and the God, the Wiccan tradition holds all life sacred. As a result, Wiccans view all human beings as children of the gods, to be treated as spiritual brothers and sisters, regardless of the paths people choose to follow on their return journey to the Divine. Wiccans are universally involved in activities aimed at increasing ecological awareness and responsibility for the earth.

Although considered a new religious movement in Canada, Wicca has been thriving for centuries. The virulent anti-paganism which made Wiccans the target of severe persecution in medieval Europe persists in North America, despite official freedom of religion. Many of the liberties associated with freedom of worship are still rather restricted. Generally, however, Wiccans in Canada practise sacred rites without fear of open reprisal, and interest in the ancient way is growing steadily, especially among those who seek alternatives to mainstream religions. In addition, Wiccans are working to ensure that their own children will increasingly be able to celebrate the fullness of a Wiccan lifestyle without fear of ridicule or harm. Children who are raised in a Wiccan environment are free to choose whatever spiritual path they feel drawn to as soon as they become adults. Wicca is not institutionalized, but there are temples in major centres across the country which are hospitable to a wide variety of inherited practices and traditions, including Gnostics, Druids, Family Traditionalists, and so on.

THE SNAKE
AND THE STONE

Niwii-debwe, Ojibway for truth, means "what is right as I know it," and storytelling is how such knowledge is shared. This view of truth among Aboriginal peoples conflicts with conventional Western beliefs that truth is absolute and objective. Increasingly, however, Western presumptions are being questioned, particularly with respect to the justice system that has so failed Native peoples.

Okimaw Ohci Healing Lodge, in Maple Creek, Saskatchewan, is an alternative to the punitive model that dominates penitentiaries. As its name implies, the Healing Lodge teaches female offenders to seek wholeness and self-respect by introducing Aboriginal values into their lives. The role of Okimaw Ohci is to enable women to assume responsibility for their actions and reintegrate into their communities.

When I first heard Brenda's voice over the phone at the Lodge, she was elated. Yes! she would write, just as she had learned to speak out. Over the next several months Brenda sent the following fragments. In one sense her story is incomplete. Yet if we're left with an unsettled edge, with more questions than answers, then perhaps the story has done its most important work.

"The Snake and the Stone" dramatizes powerfully contrasting models for reform at the Healing Lodge and the former Prison for Women at Kingston, Ontario. The opening narrative focuses on the "fast, unstable lifestyle" that landed Brenda in a life of crime. Her poetry then captures the atrocities she and others suffered at the hands of authorities in federal prison. Brenda testified before the inquiry that led to reform of the women's penal system. Her verse is included here in honour of Brenda's ongoing struggle for justice on behalf of her people. She is now a spokesperson for the Healing Lodge. Here is Brenda's truth:

The Healing Lodge has been a great inspiration to me. It's a place that has the key to healing people's lives, whether you are a criminal or a law-abiding citizen. The Lodge has its own magic, its own spiritual rules. I think we need to make the public aware of the role the Lodge plays in the prison systems, that it speaks of difference in a unique way.

My greatest gift today is my spirituality. The spirituality developed in the Healing Lodge has made me realize that I have the power to change my life and that I can understand my culture and give myself the courage to change. I now understand that in order to heal, you must let down your guard and trust the individuals who want to help you. It's amazing how you change when you are respected and trusted. I had been through the prison system and had never been treated with so much kindness and understanding. That support gives me a new balance.

Each morning at the Lodge began with a routine. First there was crying, people letting go. These sessions always ended with an elder speaking, telling a story or something to make people laugh. One story, in particular, stands out in my mind:

There was a little boy, a very young boy, who wanted to do a sweat, so he went to speak to the elders. The elders told him he had to climb the mountain. "When you get to the top," they said, "you will meet two friends. But you will have to make a choice before you can perform the sweat."

So the boy climbed the mountain, and when he got to the top, he met a snake and a stone. The boy was very young; he was not really aware of the situation he was walking into. He turned to the snake, and the snake was ready for him.

"Pick me up," the snake said to the boy. And when the boy picked it up, the snake turned into a needle and drugs. "Carry me the rest of the way and put me on that stone," the snake continued.

"But you'll bite me," the boy said.

"You knew that when you picked me up," the snake answered.

So that boy had to make a decision whether to go with the snake or not. He had to purify himself before he could do the sweat.

I listened to that story and I knew—I also have a choice.

I grew up in a fast, unstable lifestyle. I watched my parents fight and drink and separate. I then stayed with my father and went to school on Sakimay, but I was at the age where I needed both parents. Soon my father met a new lady, and they ended up living together. There were alcohol and abuses when they had parties. I would watch the parties and see the drinkers get drunker. This led to fights between my dad and stepmom. While George Jones and Tammy Wynette were playing in the background, people would pass out, not knowing what was going on. I was happier when the fighting stopped because things would go smoother. I was a proud little girl, and sometimes I would get the cold beers and open them for the drinkers. I looked after the drunks and played at the same time. I dreaded the weekends.

My father always made sure that I went to school, but by then I was fighting and not doing my school work. At this time my stepmom also started to abuse me, beating me with shoes, broomsticks, and belts. The abuse happened while my father was at work, and I did not say anything because I knew I would only get more. To make a long story short, my father stayed with this woman for several years, and they had five children together. Alcohol played a role all those years, and I lost brothers and sisters to the white people because of it.

Eventually, my mother came back into the picture, and when I was seven, she asked my dad if she could take me for a visit to her house. I was to return the following Sunday for school, but she never brought me back. Instead, she kept saying, "Next week we'll take you home." The weeks got longer and longer, and soon after I was going to school in Wilcox. I stayed on a farm with my mom and her white boyfriend. Things were pretty good at the time. I had new friends, and there was no alcohol around, and I wasn't beaten. But within the year things started to change—my mom developed a drinking problem; it caused a lot of tension in the house, and the beating began. I tried to run away to find my father, but I could not; I was too small to understand where I was or where to go. I had no choice but to keep living with my mother and keep on trying to be happy. Things got worse the next year. My mother tried to shoot her boyfriend through a kitchen window. He forgave her because she was drunk and didn't remember—the same way she didn't remember how many beatings a day I got.

My schooling dropped again, and I started to fight with the teachers and students. A new life started at age ten. My mother and I were on a bus to Regina. The man she had lived with could not handle her drinking anymore, so we were moving to the big city. Things seemed pretty exciting at the time. I didn't have to go to school right away because my mother didn't have a place yet. Our stuff stayed at the bus depot, and my mother sailed off to the bar. I waited in the restaurant. I ate my food, and the hours got longer and longer. Finally, I realized it was dark, and my mom was drunk and staggering around. I played while she was in bars, waiting in the lobbies, watching drunk people leave. I saw couples fight and get kicked out. I was hungry and tired and I wanted to sleep. Finally, there she was, staggering in front of me, holding twelve beer in her hand and calling me to follow her upstairs with her drunk friends. I listened to her friends party all night. All I cared about at that time was following my mom and watching over her and trying to get something to eat.

My mom began to drink every day, and she would forget me at nights. And I would have to wait until the bars opened to find her. Usually, the find wasn't rewarding.

I lived like this until I was apprehended by social services at age eleven. I was put in a group home called Dale House, then another one called Sedly, and from there I was sent to Prince Albert group home. By age sixteen I was home with my father on Sakimay. Slowly I started getting in trouble with the law, until I hit a jail called Pine Grove. The impact of being sent away from my family wasn't bad enough; I had hit rock bottom and was sentenced to four years in Kingston. I did about three years there and didn't learned anything because I was trying to follow the con code that prisoners follow.

I was released from Kingston and stayed out of jail for about four-and-a-half years. During that time I got into a bad drug habit and hit prison again. There I was, sailing back again to Kingston, leaving my family who needed me. But nothing could be done. I had committed a crime, and I knew that I was going away. The judge sentenced me to five years. Back to Kingston. There I lived the worst life ever and paid the price of becoming a victim myself.

The following verse is excerpted from a poem about Brenda's experience at Kingston's Prison for Women in 1994, where she and other inmates were brutalized and denigrated. After the incident was made public, a federal inquiry was initiated that resulted in national reform of the women's penal system.

There I sat, alone, Inside my own Prison
Waiting for someone to walk by or
to give me a sign of hope
With no daylight around me, I started to cry
silently to myself
Then slowly, I started to think about my
pathetic life and I wanted to scream
"I hate you, I hate you all, I hate you all"...
but no words came out.
My cell is dark and cold, and I hurt with
the pain I feel and see
At times my cell encloses around me,
and I can't breathe or think.

My feelings are wrapped by the cold air, and
my mind races with panic, as I know
They are coming.
The fear of that panic grabbed hold of me.
In an instant
It brought darkness. It began to happen.
The men were there, they were coming to me
With no fear and no shame.
I waited and waited like a nervous child,
who was once scared of the dark
My heart was going faster than the winds
outside as I began to realize
That they were there, and it was happening,
dark masked men banged on my cell door,
wearing shields of ignorance and pain.
It showed behind their shadows and in their
voices of ignorance.
In seconds, a thousand thoughts raced through
my mind of what was about to happen.
My body and mind went into shock as they
told me to kneel with my hands behind my
head
And they told me no harm would come to me.
I asked if there were any women here.
But little did they know that the harm was
already done
from hearing the screams of others and
hearing their pain and cries of shame.
Some would even try to laugh
to hide the pain.
I remember I gave a burst of laughter.
Slowly, I felt the men's hands all over me,
wrapping the cold chains
Around my body and feet and hands.
Felt the pain and the humiliation
As I was wrapped with chains and torn
with humiliation.
I was being degraded in front of white men.

Laughed at by Corrections—Corrections,
who held control of my life...
I was sorry for breaking the law, I was sorry
that I could be treated that way
For I know in my heart that the judge did not
sentence me to this kind of treatment
inside a prison. I wonder if he knew that he
had let this happen to me. I wonder if he
approved of this kind of treatment.
I wonder if he called this sexual assault...
I asked myself, do I give up my life to help
others or do I live to help others
The pain still wears inside my mind.
The flashes of Corrections stay.
The wounds have not even begun to heal.
For I still feel victimized by the hands of
Corrections...
So please don't hurt us anymore
We can love like you love,
we can cry like you cry
we can feel pain like you feel pain, we are
human like you.
So please take your chains off me now,
so I can feel human again.
Give me back my clothes, so I can wear them
without shame
close the windows, so I can feel the warmth
I once felt
give me a shower so I can wash off the men's
hands that hurt me
please don't hurt me anymore please don't
hurt us anymore...
Something had made me see how wicked the
government can be
when given so much power over people's lives
My eyes have seen and witnessed the horror
of Corrections.

But I will not let it kill me
I will try to be a leader for the love of my
people
The love that I have for people who are under
the lock and key of Corrections
The understanding, knowing the pain that a
prisoner goes through
Under the hands of Corrections.
Yes, that's right what you're thinking,
Corrections do need to change their ways
There is no end to this story of pain
But there is love
I forgive you for what you have done to me
I will use this as a tool for my own benefit
For the love I now hold in my heart, for the
love of my people and prisoners.

Brenda Acoose Morrison
Grenfell, Saskatchewan

"Existing law is not the solution. Tradition is the solution. Recovering our distinct ways of being is the solution." The pointed words of Mohawk writer, lawyer, and educator, Patricia Monture-Angus, speak directly to the tensions between Canadian and Aboriginal models for justice.

First Nations men, women, and youth have been criminalized and incarcerated in Canada's prisons for over a century. Now, however, Aboriginal peoples are asserting the desire to regain control of their own criminal law matters.

Efforts to heal the disproportionate numbers of Native peoples trapped in Canada's corrections system raise the need for Aboriginal self-determination. At the heart of Aboriginal justice proposals are spirituality and healing. Traditional values focus on harmony, balance, and the connectedness of all things, meaning retribution is replaced by peacemaking. Peacemaking in First Nations communities means listening closely and choosing a course of action that brings offenders back into harmony with others. Justice arises from the collective wisdom of the community. Patience and attunement guide this process; stories bring it to life.

Among Aboriginal peoples storytelling is regarded as a primary means of teaching and law-giving. Stories encourage and nourish, they embody values and impart examples that show how people are expected to live. Stories focus on the consequences of actions, and listeners are free to draw their own conclusions. In this way people are invited to find their own meaning and their own truth. In this lies the beginning of wisdom.

THE BURNING MOUNTAIN

The first Buddhist scripture I read was the Fire Sermon, one of the initial sermons Shakyamuni delivered after becoming Buddha under the World Tree over twenty-five hundred years ago. Perhaps the first widely known sutra in the West, the sermon was most likely delivered to monks near an active volcano not far from Benares. Amidst earth tremors and smoke the Buddha did something quite typical. He turned to his followers and said, "This reminds me of a sermon:"

> *I am pleased to be present in this sacred place with you. This place here, where we sit together, has become sacred because of our meeting together in the spirit of trust and wisdom sharing. The fact that we are*

*gathered here in this circle in that spirit is of great
significance for our futures. Because…we have the
opportunity to change the flow of our karma.
The flow of our lives and the life of our community is a
stream of events that leads back into the infinite past
and forward into the infinite future. Because we have
had the courage to meet within the sacred circle of
trust and wisdom sharing, we can now change the
nature of that stream of events. From this sacred place
we have created here we can observe the world clearly.
And what do we see when we look out upon the world
from the vantage point of trust and wisdom sharing?
We see that the whole world is burning.*

My ancestors were Quaker, Old German Baptist, and United
Brethren, people who believed there were alternatives more
beneficial to the human community than repression and blind
obedience. Not surprisingly, they were asked by politicians and
church officials, sometimes impolitely, to leave their homeland,
and between 1850 and 1950 family members streamed out of
Germany by the hundreds. Once in North America they gravitated
towards like-minded groups and intermarried with First Nations
tribes, mainly Oneida, Winnebago, and Cherokee. One branch,
the Baileys, lived in Manitoba's Red River colony and took part in
Louis Riel's rebellion.

History caught up with us eventually. After Riel it was thought
disgraceful to be Native, and after the world wars there was great
shame in being German. Though some of my uncles broke faith
with the peace churches to fight in the old country, they were still
rejected by mainstream theology. Some relatives still practised the
old ways of the First Nations people, but at that time Native
spirituality was not even a topic of serious discussion.

*Everything is on fire. What do we mean when we say,
"The whole world is being consumed by flames?" We
mean the world is burning with the fires of ignorance.
The world beyond this sacred place is ablaze with
hatred. The world beyond trust and wisdom sharing is*

aflame with greed.... The whole world beyond this
sacred place of trust and wisdom sharing is ablaze,
burning out of control, a conflagration! And how do
human beings react to this turmoil?

After graduating from university, I left for Iliff School of Theology in Denver, Colorado. I felt great relief as I glimpsed the Rocky Mountains and the city of Denver. After all, just how far can marginalization carry? Every idea, theology, and identity I tried had failed me. I had always sought the answers to my religious striving within the Christian community, which sometimes led to spiritual gymnastics. I'd been campus religious leader, pastor of a small Methodist church, and student pastor in a large one. Many back home were disappointed by my choice of schools and regarded Iliff as the first step towards atheism. For me, however, Iliff was the first step towards spiritual authenticity.

The breakthrough came when I took a library job cataloguing the entire works of Albert Schweitzer. Schweitzer talked about Christian values and theology without using the words Jesus, Christ, God, or the Bible. I entered this gateway with the joy of decontextualization—what Buddhists call "the shimmering void." At last I realized that obedience, submission, guilt, blame, and shame were not primary religious experiences. Christian rhetoric could be transcended without violating deep spiritual truths. Other linguistic networks could reveal the same truths in other contexts. Schweitzer's approach made my search for spiritual authenticity possible.

I then began to contact many churches and religious leaders in earnest. After I attended the Denver Buddhist Temple, it became clear that the solution to my spiritual quest was not in texts but in the vortex of direct experience. I planned a vision quest.

Some people shout, screaming, "Bring more
wood!"...Others shout, screaming, "We need more
carpenters."...Still other voices shout, screaming, "The
fire is an illusion."...Another group shouts, screaming,
"We will hear no negative anecdotes." They watch and
watch and watch, through closed eyes. Meanwhile, the

world smoulders, covered with soot....

The firestorm of ignorance, hatred, and greed offers great opportunities. Some will become rich by selling us water in small containers at high prices. Some will call us to worship the fire. Some will call us to escape the fire through delusion. Some will call us to escape through entertainment. Some will tell us to ignore it and it will go away. Others will call us simply to enjoy the fire.

The Buddha has a different message, however.

I chose a spot up Boulder Canyon—nine days in the forest, plus a few days to prepare and a few days to assimilate what I had learned. Meals were scanty. The time not spent meditating, I spent walking. There was such a sense of being alive that sleep didn't seem necessary; when it did come, it was deep and rejuvenating. There were conversations with animals, birds, and trees. Everything was communicating with me.

I'd been sitting for some time under a large pine tree when I heard a sob. It was a deep-throated sob, like what might escape a child in a bomb raid. The mother was sobbing and trying to breastfeed a dead baby, as if she hoped her milk would bring the baby back to life. This sob was coming from the ground beneath me. I searched behind the tree and under the car, even on the road a little distance away. After returning to the tree, I heard the sob again. Then Mother Earth spoke to me.

She told me many things, some of which I cannot put into words. We are killing the earth, and she must soon decide what to do. We are her favourite creation. Our species has evolved to become life-givers, capable of transforming suffering into higher spiritual and moral power. There have been many mass deaths throughout earth's history; now, at last, by means of human consciousness, life can survive indefinitely. But something has gone wrong. A nihilistic neurosis has infected the human brain, and she, the earth, must soon decide whether to trust us or to limit our numbers so that we do not threaten the continuation of life on earth. We will be given one last chance at spiritual regeneration. Religions that emphasize submission and obedience and the denigration of non-human life forms will have to change; so too will economic patterns that rob the environment and give nothing in return. Mother Earth then finished with the phrase that marks so many First Nation vision quests, "Carry out your days in simplicity and humility, and as a relative to all that lives."

> *This is what the Buddha says; he says "Call the fire department!...The world is burning. Help put out the fires!"*
>
> *We are born into a world where no one escapes old age, sickness, and death....Sometimes we have to fight in armies....Sometimes we have to do violence to protect our families....Why add the scourge of fire to this, our world? But it has been done! Thus we live in samsara. Twisting, turning, rising, falling, cycling, and recycling the world of attachments, delusion, and craving.*

The sobbing would not stop, so I jumped in the car and returned to Denver, leaving the camping gear behind. There could be no return to that particular spot until I had strength enough to listen to the sobbing again. Surely it is there still, waiting for those who have ears to hear it. From that time on I was determined to live my life in such a way that when I did return, the sobbing would have abated.

That first Sunday of my re-entry, I attended the Denver Buddhist Temple. The congregation was chanting, *"Namu Amida Buddha,"* which Reverend Tsunoda explained as, "'My mind is full of infinite life and infinite light.' It is reverence for life on a grand scale."

Twenty years later as bishop of the Buddhist Churches of Canada, Revered Tsunoda sponsored me for ordination into the Buddhist priesthood. I had come to Canada from Frankfurt to study comparative historical linguistics, renew my Métis heritage, and explore the area near my grandfather's homestead near Medicine Hat. The occasion was the eightieth anniversary of the introduction of Buddhism into Canada.

Soon we will be celebrating our centennial. I am grateful I will be alive to join in the celebrations. The dharma has given me the freedom to experience the sacred energy that is the basis of all things and has allowed for integration of all the disparate elements of my background. The dharma, which is remarkably similar to First Nations spirituality, does not reject other religions but represents accumulative, inclusive wisdom. It is a privilege to be part of a pioneer generation that is revealing the dharma in Canada.

> *But this day, today, is special. The place we share this morning has become a sacred place because we occupy it this morning by the act of trust and wisdom sharing. Now that we are in a sacred place, our ears are prepared to hear dharma, the sustaining spiritual force that uplifts us and gives us hope...*
>
> Translated by Fred Ulrich

Fred Ulrich
Winnipeg, Manitoba

Although representing only a small percentage of Buddhists across the country, Pure Land comprises one of the largest schools of Buddhism in the world. In Canada there are about sixteen groups nationwide; Alberta alone has six temples. Pure Land Buddhism was probably the first form of organized Buddhism introduced into Canada. Many Chinese who worked on the railroads were Buddhist. Although as far as we know, they did not possess a formal organization, many would likely have been Pure Land adherents.

Pure Land's popularity throughout the Buddhist world is due partly to its straightforward message that all beings may achieve salvation through faith in the compassion of Amida Buddha. Assured of buddhahood, or paradise (Pure Land), devotees concentrate on a life of humble service and gratitude. As the religion of the people, Pure Land eschews the rigours favoured by other Buddhist paths (Rinzai Zen, for example) in favour of simple practices accessible to all. The rights of women, laypeople, the poor, and Aboriginal peoples are all championed by Pure Land.

Buddhism originated in India in the fifth and sixth centuries BCE and eventually made its way to China via travelling monks. In

China Buddhism attracted followers from all sectors of society; the Pure Land and Ch'an (Zen) schools were especially popular. In the fifth or sixth century CE, Buddhism entered Japan, and further refinements developed. One of these was the Jodoshinshu school, or Shin Buddhism, developed by Shinran (d. 1262) some eight hundred years ago. Shinran's insights into the Pure Land tradition emphasized devotion over austere spiritual practice. The Shin mother temple is in Kyoto.

The first adherents of Shin Buddhism arrived in Canada in 1833; by 1905 a temple had been established in Vancouver. Over the years Japanese immigration brought more and more lay people who were loyal to their faith despite strong social pressures. Shin Buddhists have survived relentless pressures to convert, internment during World War II, and a 60 percent intermarriage rate with the general Canadian population. The Japanese Buddhist community, which has shown such strong mutual support among members, extends that support to the whole of Canadian society in the quiet, persistent intent to contribute to its betterment.

Buddhism, however, also appeals to non-Asians and is now the fastest growing religion in North America. The attraction to Shin is no exception in this respect. Shin's simple doctrines, egalitarian culture, and democratic structures bode well for its future in Canada. Pure Land Buddhism celebrates its Canadian centennial in the year 2005.

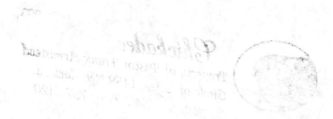

JAINISM:
Promise of a Peaceful Twenty-first Century

My spiritual journey into Jainism began earnestly in Canada some thirty-five years ago. I was teaching chemistry at a university in British Columbia, when a fellow professor from religious studies asked me to speak to her class on Jainism. Someone had told her that I was a Jain. She had also noticed that I was vegetarian, showed somewhat extra sensitivity to the plight of plants and animals, and treated the ecosystem around me with rather unusual reverence. In the context of North American norms of the sixties, this was rather odd behaviour.

To me, however, this marked sensitivity was simply the way I had been reared as a child. It was only later, as a scientist, that I was taught to be logical and skeptical. I had very little understanding of the religious and ethical principles that had shaped my life.

Certainly, I was a skeptic as far as religious faith was concerned, and since most religions demand belief (a form of blind faith, as far as I was concerned), religion had no validity in my life.

As it turns out, this invitation to speak on Jainism prompted me to explore the philosophical and ethical basis of my own lifestyle. Until then I had neither seen nor read any Jain literature. So when I received my first book from India on Jainism—an English translation of an eleventh-century commentary on Jain scripture—I attacked it with a blend of scientific curiosity, skepticism, and critical analysis. The *Dravya-Sangraha* was a treat for a scientist's logical, analytical mind. There were the suprises in store for me.

The opening verse salutes the Jain *Tirthankaras* (spiritual teachers) for revealing that everything in the universe is either *jiva* (soul energy), or *pudgala* (matter), or a result of these. The book quickly moves on to state that these two, that is, energy and matter, together with space, time, motion, and inertia are the fundamental and eternal substances of the universe. Being eternal, they can neither be created nor destroyed. However, mutual interaction or inter-conversions are possible.

With terms such as matter, energy, time, space, and so on, this ancient religious scripture read like a modern scientific treatise. Interconvertibility and interaction between matter and energy (Einstein's key contribution) are supposed to be the scientific discovery of the twentieth century. Eternity of matter and energy, concepts of space, time, motion, inertia—aren't these what modern physics is all about? I had to read the book over and over, and each time I was awed by its scientific insight.

Yet this text was merely a commentary on a much earlier work. The Tattvartha Sutra (A Manual for Understanding All That Is) encapsulated the religious, ethical, and philosophical contents of Jain scriptures, yet it did not demand blind faith, promise mercy for the faithful, or threaten the infidel. Neither did the work assert a singular truth. The author, philosopher-monk Umaswati, warned against accepting anything as gospel: any statement, regardless of either its authority or logical, factual, or emotional appeal, could be only a partial and relative truth. Absolute truth, the sutra maintained, is beyond human comprehension. What I found was a reasoned, logical appeal to the intellect, asking repeatedly that only those arguments that met the reader's highest intellectual and critical scrutiny be accepted. To my mind this sounded like a five-thousand-year-old affirmation of modern scientific thinking. On reading further, I actually discovered the basis for much of my own behaviour and worldview explained in this second century philosophical treatise.

The Tattvartha Sutra summarizes the central themes of the scriptures regarding the Jain code of conduct as conditioning one's mind for non-violence, non-absolutism, and non-possession. The philosophical basis for such a code is that life in all forms, shapes, and sizes has soul energy that is essentially the same, whether it appears in humans, plants, or animals; soul energy sustains every living being. Every soul, I read, is eternal and potentially omniscient and omnipotent. Therefore, every life must be preserved, respected, and revered. This Jain concept of soul energy as the essential element of all forms of life strengthens the autonomy of every living being and has made non-violence, or *ahimsa,* the central Jain doctrine; hence the basis for my own and my fellow Jains' vegetarianism.

Beyond prescribing non-violence, the Jain text advocated asceticism and the practice of inquiry. It was this promotion of inquiry through non-absolutism that resonated so deeply with my own life choice to become a scientist. According to the Jain doctrine of non-absolutism, or *anekta,* all knowledge other than omniscience is only partial truth from a particular viewpoint. Non-absolutism strengthens the autonomy of thought of every individual and promotes active investigation as a means of broadening one's knowledge, understanding, and exploration of truth.

Here, then, was the basis not only for understanding a scientific mind but also for finding hope that some of the gravest problems plaguing the planet at that time might be solved. Non-absolutism was a tool to ensure against dogmatism—what to my mind was the root of human conflict. The days when my professor friend launched me on the path of personal spiritual quest were also the days of environmental awakening, the Vietnam war, flower-power, and dropping out of the rat race. North America was warming up to the messages of peace, non-violence, racial equality, and human dignity. The morality of blind faith in the name of nationalism, religion, or ideology was being questioned. Ironically, I was finding these same modern issues prophetically addressed in the old Jain scriptures.

The practice of asceticism, or living humbly, also helped me to understand the environmental consciousness I had observed within the Jain community. The doctrine of non-possession, or *aprigraha*, asks Jains to limit their possessions and live harmoniously in a state of interdependence with the entire ecosystem:

> *He who knows what is bad for himself knows what is bad for others, and he who knows what is bad for others knows what is bad for himself. One whose mind is at peace and who is free from passions does not desire to live at the expense of others. He who understands the nature of sin against earth, water, air, fire, plants and animals is a true sage and understands karma. For, all these elements are truly alive (possess soul energy) and those who harm them, harm themselves by bonding their souls firmly with non-liberating karma.*

> Acharang Sutra, 600 BCE

Now it is one thing to lay down principles, and quite another to ensure that generations to come will live by them. The Jain masters achieved this by blending spirituality with practice. They taught that every soul has the potential to liberate itself from the painful cycle of birth and death and to attain a pure state, *moksha,* in which the soul is omniscient, omnipotent, and enjoys eternal bliss. Rishabha, the first *Tirthankara,* showed the path to *moksha* more than five thousand years ago, when he revealed that the secret lies in winning complete victory (*jit*) over one's emotions, passions, desires, and weaknesses. Such victory, or winning over the self, is gained by practising self-discipline through meditation, inquiry, and austerity. Those who have achieved such victory are called *jina.* A Jain is one who follows the path showed by *jina.*

Jains have absorbed and retained this code of conduct for thousands of years. Today a vegetarian committed to peace and goodwill among all creatures is no longer regarded as odd. Though

Jainism's ancient religious and philosophical history is still little known in the West, more North Americans are being exposed to the Jain way of living. Increasingly, they realize that Jains are upholding their most fundamental principles when they advocate non-violence towards all beings, showing unusual sensitivity towards the plight of plants and animals, and treating the ecosystem with reverence.

Twenty-five hundred years ago during the time of Mahavira (the last *Tirthankara*) practising the principles of non-violence, non-absolutism, and non-possession was seen to be the only means of achieving personal and social peace. In the years since I began my own journey into Jainism, I have come to realize that this philosophy is even more relevant today. The world has not changed much since the early sixties. Deadly acts of war, economic exploitation, and environmental degradation are still with us. What is different, however, is my absence of equanimity. Jainism offers me solutions, and in solutions lie hope.

This hope has made me pro-active; not that I want to proselytize Jainism, but I do want to promote its values. Practical solutions for saving our planet, as well as our souls, are available to us through the values Jains have lived by for millennia. Now if only the rest of the world embraced these values as we entered the new millennium! Jains hope that one day the world will in fact adopt these as universal human values. Perhaps in so doing, our planet will finally find the promise of peace, as I have, for the twenty-first century.

Vastupal Parikh
Brampton, Ontario

Jainism is an ancient religion with about fifteen million followers, mostly in India. Primarily an ethical religion, Jainism focuses on moral conduct rather than theology. The root of Jain philosophy may be traced to ascetic traditions of the Indus Valley (India–Pakistan) over five thousand years ago. These traditions developed practices aimed at disciplining the mind and eliminating its weaknesses: ego, lust, prejudice, greed, desire, and so on. Rishabha, whom Jains regard as the first of their twenty-four spiritual teachers, advocated a lifestyle involving contemplation, meditation, and austerity. Faithful adherence to this way of life allowed an individual to gain control over the mind and to reach the state of absolute bliss, thereby liberating the soul from the painful cycles of birth and rebirth.

Mahavira, who was a contemporary of Buddha, was a reformer and the last of the Jain great spiritual teachers. Mahavira committed ascetic principles and practices to twelve main scriptures or Agamas. For centuries Jains have followed Mahavira's Code of Conduct in the pursuit of internal peace and liberation.

Jains have enriched Indian culture through scholarship, literature, art, architecture, and sculpture, and Jain temples in India rank among the world's finest. The philosophy of non-violence and non-absolutism has enabled Jainism to avoid conflicts and remain peaceful during religious upheavals throughout the long history of India.

Jains began settling in North America about forty years ago, and their current number is estimated at around fifty thousand. There are eighty-five Jain centres in North America, thirteen of them in Canada. Toronto's is one of the largest, with about one thousand Jain families. Other centres may be found in Vancouver, Edmonton, London, Ottawa, and Montreal.

HELEN AND HUMANISM

Prometheus was the only one in the council of the gods
who favoured man. He alone was kind to the human
race, and taught and protected them. Jupiter, angry at
the insolence and presumption of Prometheus,
...condemned the Titan to perpetual imprisonment,
bound to a rock on Mount Caucasus while a vulture
should forever prey upon his liver.

Thomas Bulfinch, Mythology

Considering the words "neighbour" and "faith" in the title of this book, the point could be made that someone in Canada could not have a neighbour in far-distant China, and that someone brought up in mainland communist China would not likely have a faith. Yet Helen was my neighbour in Shaanxi's Xi'an, where I lived and taught seven years ago, and the communism in which she was raised could be considered a faith. The classical Helen was the cause of the Trojan war; my Chinese neighbour, Helen (for such was her English name), precipitated if not a war then certainly a pointed re-evaluation of cultural assumptions I had long taken for granted. And more—she was also the occasion for wonder: how could such a bright person not understand a certain Canadian journal I wanted her to read?

Helen was the well-comprehending young monitor in one of my literature courses. In China monitors tend to be chosen by their fellow students to act, for example, as intermediaries between teacher and students in cases of conflict. I could see that, with Helen, they had chosen well. She lived with her parents in an apartment building near mine; her father was a faculty member, in science.

The first time I noticed Helen, I had been in my apartment less than a week, the torrid summer weather had started to abate, and she went bicycling by below my windows. I had been busying myself with teaching preparation and was then surprised when I stepped into my night class that very evening to see the same young woman come forward, all smiles, to introduce herself as the monitor.

Her duties were to be well performed. On that muggy evening the windows stood wide open to admit air, light bulbs glared down fiercely, and the room was alive with multitudes of insects, some nearly the size of small birds, which darted about, batting against walls and blackboards as I strove to speak to the class. Helen came up at the end of the hour to say that though the bugs were distressing, she knew from past years the invaders would soon be gone. Her gracious gesture was welcome; her prediction proved correct.

In October Helen told me she had a small paid project translating Chinese into English. She wanted me to advise her on some fine points, and I agreed, inviting her to my place the next afternoon. I had made my corrections and she was leaving when she spied contributors' copies of *Humanist in Canada* on my desk. I then explained I was a Humanist. Partly to further acquaint her with Canada, I handed her a copy of the journal, suggesting she might borrow it. She would be glad to she said. I sensed she would read through it carefully.

Not long after—following a Halloween party staged by foreign teachers—Helen told me she wished to see me again to return the journal and have a conversation. Again we decided on the following afternoon, and when she rang the bell, I was making tea. Once seated, she looked through the pages. "I have read it all," she began. "But I do not understand Humanism."

Knowing her astute grasp of things, I found this remark baffling. "You do not like it or dislike it," I offered. "You just don't understand it."

She nodded.

"Of course, you know something about the ancient Greeks," I added.

"A little," she answered.

"They had a group of gods called Titans, of whom Prometheus was one," I continued. "He is very important to Humanists, because he took fire from the gods and their mighty leader, Zeus, or Jupiter, as the ancient Romans called him. Prometheus gave this fire to humanity for their use. For this he was terribly punished."

"But was it a good thing for him to do, to take the fire?" she queried.

"Of course," I said summarily. "With fire humanity made such progress."

"But he stole it," Helen replied. "And it is wrong to steal."

I had never before heard this said about Prometheus. "The gods had plenty more fire," I pointed out, rather baldly.

"But Prometheus should have asked permission," she added.

"I don't think he would have been given permission," I countered.

"Then he would have to hope he would and try hard," she pronounced.

I realized that Helen was disturbed at the thought of stealing, regardless of how noble the cause. In China—at least then—it was said you were supposed to give money found on the street to the nearest police officer. But something else was troubling Helen. "He should not have acted alone like that," she explained.

"But it was for the good of humanity," I exclaimed. By this

point I was rather astonished at the direction the discussion had taken.

Yes, that was important, Helen conceded, then refined her point: "But I think Prometheus should have tried to act together with the whole council of the gods."

I tried to picture the gods of Mount Olympus behaving like a People's Committee, which seemed precisely what Helen thought they ought to have done. She continued, "If they had all gone to Zeus for his permission, I think Zeus would have given it. Zeus is like our Chairman Mao Tse Tung," she laughed.

"Of course," I said, trying a different tack, "the ancient Greeks had these gods, but in time they were dropped. Humanists have no gods, and neither do you today in the People's Republic."

She was not to be won over so easily. "But," Helen reasoned, "taking fire like that was wrong because Prometheus stole and acted alone."

I felt her points were legitimate. It seemed, then, that there was a bad Prometheus and a good Prometheus, the first a thief and the second, like Jesus, a saviour. Humanists, of course, dote on the good Prometheus. During the course of history had he been turned into a Christian? Helen was helping me to recognize this discrepancy for the first time.

I asked if she had trouble understanding Humanism because of her problem with Prometheus. "No," she answered. "I had never heard of him before you mentioned him."

"Then why is it hard for you to follow things in this journal?" I was altogether puzzled at her conclusion. She did her best to clarify her position, which amounted to the fact that she just could not see what all the fuss was about. I pressed the matter further. "Does it seem unnecessary for people to write such things?" I asked.

"Yes, I think so," she replied. I could not follow her logic, and the conversation drew to a close.

Only later after she left, did the likely reason for Helen's attitude dawn on me. In the West modern-day Humanists have taken a cue from the ancient saying, "Man is the measure of all things," throwing critical darts at God and religious traditions, especially Christianity, in the name of science and reason. Canadian

Humanism has gone along in much this way and engaged in what are sometimes called negative polemics. But in China with the revolution, religions were officially discouraged, if not banished, with the result that they ceased being a mainstream target. Hence in China Western Humanism seemed superfluous, something of a fish out of water. Was this the reason for Helen's lack of comprehension?

Then again, I could also see the Humanist truths in Marxism—so far as they went. Likewise, I could see how countries everywhere want to dub themselves democracies—from Lenin's "New Democracy" (the dictatorship of the proletariat), to Canada, the United States, and England. But as a teacher in China, I sometimes had to swallow my Humanism in private conversation, trying to encourage freedom of conscience in religious matters among students who were seeking my advice while they were being hounded by the state. Such students, unlike Helen, were given no clues as to my Humanism. Had I loaned them Humanist journals, the students would likely have been just as puzzled and uncomprehending.

The year on campus moved along and wound down in spring for final exams but not before a class party. We played a few amusing games and listened to our monitor make a short speech thanking me on behalf of the class. All of us basked in her smile. My last glimpse of Helen was where I had first seen her—capably wheeling along the path below my windows in slacks and a T-shirt, her hair cropped short for summer.

What I didn't know as she cycled past was that, seven years later, I would re-create our afternoon conversation on Humanism. Helen gave me a photo of her taken in winter in front of a new gate—an image more perfectly detailed perhaps than this reconstruction. Still, the latter is no less clearly etched in memory.

David Lawson
Westmount, Quebec

The journal, *Humanist in Canada*, describes itself on its cover page as "challenging established beliefs." Provoking active and informed discussion regarding the betterment of society is an express goal of The Canadian Humanist Association, chapters of which may be found in cities throughout Canada.

The Humanist tradition traces its roots to the pagan classical world of Greece and Rome. Renaissance Humanism, emerging after the long monastic period in Western civilization, declared that the best exemplification of human ideals was to be found in the Greek and Roman classics. This emphasis meant a less religious, more down-to-earth approach, as can be found in Petrarch and Boccaccio.

Modern pragmatic Humanism derives from late nineteenth-century America. Canadian Humanists, in particular, bear the influence of English empiricism, logical positivism, and American pragmatism. Some of the most forward-looking and creative thinkers, including Bertrand Russell, Baruch Spinoza, and Karl Marx, all took Humanist positions at one time or another. (Accordingly, Chinese Marxism has Humanist influences.)

Humanists champion independent thinking and freedom of choice over divine revelation, miracles, or faith claims. Religious ritual and belief systems are viewed as detractors from the basic work of creating a sound society. Nevertheless, insofar as a humane and just society is sought, religion and Humanism share a common goal.

WALKING THE RIVERBANK

Like most adult Unitarian Universalists, I wasn't born into the faith. I came out of another tradition, in my case, Roman Catholicism. Becoming a Unitarian is really an adult decision, even for those born into the church, and a choice based as much on reason as on faith or intuition. This emphasis on choice is significant, since Unitarianism emerged from the Protestant Reformation and the Enlightenment that followed as a reason-based approach to religion. Above all else, our faith must make sense to us.

That said, the role of intuition is also an important part of Unitarianism, for intuition often sends a truer and deeper message than the reasoning intellect. Put another way, the heart sometimes knows the truth before the head catches on. There are different ways of knowing, especially when it comes to knowing oneself, and each of these ways must be explored to help us discern our truth.

Perhaps that's why I've always loved stories. They tell truths in an intuitive and emotional way. Stories speak directly to the heart, often bypassing the head completely. We resonate with a story that speaks to us, long before our intellects have time to process its moral or meaning.

Unitarians have no sacred scriptures of their own but respect other traditions and look to each for its particular store of teachings—and stories—in forming their faith statements. We find that most religions try to teach the same essential truths but express them in different ways.

A pivotal story in my own spiritual formation comes from the Hebrew scriptures, that of Jacob wrestling with the angel. Now here was a bad egg, a dishonourable man who had cheated his brother, Esau, out of his birthright and taken advantage of their father in the process. Not surprisingly, Esau swore he'd kill Jacob. Neither hero nor fool, Jacob ran away and made a life for himself with his mother's family in another land.

Jacob then ingratiated himself with his uncle, who was both his boss and later father-in-law (twice! but that's another story...), and got into some shady business with sheep and goats, building up a great deal of wealth along the way. As often happens when someone is skirting the thin edge of legality, Jacob was eventually found out. Now just about this time he had a dream. And in this dream God warned Jacob that he was in danger. Jacob decided perhaps it was time to patch things up with his brother, Esau; so gathering up his family and goods, Jacob fled in the night, back to his homeland.

Free of the danger behind him, Jacob turned his thoughts to what lay ahead. He grew afraid of what Esau might do upon his return. Drawing closer to the river that marked the boundary between the two nations, Jacob sent a large gift ahead to placate Esau, then divided his own family and herds into two groups, sending these across by two separate routes. That way, at least half of his fortune would be preserved were Esau to attack.

Night fell, and Jacob was left alone with his thoughts on the riverbank. That night he would have to decide something far more important than whether or not to cross the river. He would have to choose how to live the rest of his life. Would he take responsibility? Or would he sneak away yet again?

During the night a man—some say an angel—came to Jacob, and the two began to wrestle. All night long they fought, yet neither ever gained the upper hand. Towards morning the angel touched Jacob's leg, dislocating his hip. Despite the agony Jacob wrestled on. "Let me go," the angel cried, "for day is breaking." But Jacob refused until the figure blessed him.

As the first rays of the sun crept over the horizon, the angel relented. "You shall no longer be called Jacob, but Israel," the angel pronounced. "For you have striven with God and with humans, and have prevailed."

No sooner had he said this than the angel was gone, and Jacob/Israel was left agonizing in the dust. In time he drew himself up, resolved what he had to do. Before crossing the river, he turned and looked at the place where he had wrestled with the stranger; already the desert breeze was erasing the marks of their struggle. And he named the place Peniel, which means, "I have seen God face to face, and yet my life is preserved." Then Israel turned and went forward to meet his brother and his fate.

Well, I don't think of myself as a cheat, but I have made mistakes in my life, and I have hurt people along the way. I have run away from problems that seemed too frightening. And throughout those times, this story haunted me. When I finally turned to look at it, the story taught me the value of honour. You can never fully run away from your honour, I realized. It won't let go. At some point you have to face your life, admit your failings, and reclaim your dignity and worth.

Divorce and other reversals many years ago drew me to the riverbank, a desolate place, where neither the way ahead nor the way behind held much promise. Finally, I too had to decide how I would live the rest of my life.

What I learned from Jacob is that if we have the courage to wrestle with the inner angel of self-knowledge, and if we are tenacious about that struggle even in the face of pain and suffering, we can find the answer that is right and moral and honest.

And for our efforts we will gain two things: the wounds and

scars that the honest living of life invariably inflicts and a new name, a new pride, a new sense of self that comes from having prevailed over the shadowy demons inhabiting our souls.

My Irish Catholic mother often said, "God helps those who help themselves!" That too is part of Jacob's story. Until we're ready to face ourselves, we cannot change our lot. Unitarian Universalist principles begin by affirming the inherent worth and dignity of every person, but perhaps we can only truly claim that dignity when we face up to our failings and accept our wounds as well as our strengths.

As for me, at the end of my struggles (that round, at least) I found myself wounded yet the owner of a new faith and a deeply rooted sense of calling to the ministry.

Perhaps the meaning of my story is that ministry was always the path I wanted to follow, just as Jacob always needed to face his brother. Yet we both had to run away and do some serious soul searching, some real wrestling, before we could discover the truth that was always so close to home.

By the way, Esau ran to meet his brother and embraced him.

Brian J. Kiely
Edmonton, Alberta

Unitarians, or Unitarian Universalists, trace their roots to the most radical thinkers of the Protestant Reformation. Historically two separate liberal movements, the congregations merged in 1961 to become the Unitarian Universalist Association. At one time Unitarian Universalists were considered heretical by mainstream Christian churches; today they enjoy an increased affiliation with individuals of all faiths who are committed to intellectually, emotionally, and spiritually integrated approaches to humanity and the universe.

A creedless faith, Unitarianism calls for the use of both reason and intuition to help people formulate their own beliefs. Unitarians are guided by a Statement of Principles, a democratically created document open to revision whenever the need arises. The Principles affirm the worth and dignity of all, calling for work towards justice and respect for the interdependent web of all creation.

Unitarians have no sacred text but respect all scriptures and teachings of the world's faiths. A distinctive mark of Unitarians is their willingness to investigate other traditions and examine what each contributes to the wisdom and knowledge of the world. The UUA recognizes Christianity, Humanism, Judaism, Earth-Centred traditions (such as Wicca, Native, and Afro-American religions), other world religions, and prophets as the sources of its own spiritual vision and heritage.

Part of Canada's diverse religious landscape since the 1830s, Unitarianism has active congregations in most of the country's major urban centres.

EVERY PERSON
HAS A STORY

Every person has a story; I help the most mournful, broken people write theirs.

These people left parts of their souls behind in the death camps of Europe. They are the Jewish victims of the Holocaust, people who started out in life just the way we start out. They grew up in families, rich or poor, in towns in Poland or large cities in Germany, France, and Hungary. Some were from religious homes; some, from homes that had long ago forgotten age-old traditions.

Mr. A. is a survivor. He is compelled to write his story over and over in a variety of literary forms. His story was set on stage. He has written two autobiographies, commemorating and mourning his family who died before their time. Now he writes poetry, creating the same images again and again obsessively. There was a time when I listened to his story and edited the written account. He would appear at my door, a sheaf of papers in his hands, week after week. Most of what was written would be coherent, hindered only by his non-native English. But the last pages of the poems were wildly written in angry handwriting. He never had time to complete a clean draft before bringing me the manuscript. Sometimes on the way to my study, final words were scrawled on the backs of bus transfers.

We would drink tea together—that was all; he was too religious to trust my standards of kosher cooking. He was quiet and modest, with a respectful demeanour that belied his fury and the memories of tortures he had experienced in Europe. He would read his shocking life out loud to me, and I would gaze out the window, watching cars go by, watching the snow fall, watching normal lives pass by.

His life too had once been normal. He must have been a cute blond child in Poland in the twenties and thirties. But normalcy betrayed him, sent his life careening into the most bizarre, horrible nightmare. When the Nazis invaded his native town in Poland, his father, a rabbi, told his young blond son to run away, to hide his identity. Somehow, he escaped the town and attached himself to a unit in the Polish army. Somehow, despite his Yiddish accent, despite his circumcision, he managed to evade detection as a Jew. He watched his fellow Jews die and never forgave himself for not turning himself in. He worked for the underground, for the partisans, helping Jews escape whenever he could. And when the Russian army finally arrived in Poland, Mr. A. begged them for mercy. Alas, they didn't believe him and threw him into prison. It took months to convince the Russians he was a Jew.

The rest of Mr. A's life has been a horrid nightmare. The screams, the indecision, the memories of death marches and cattle cars carrying Jews just like him haunt him still. The realization that his innocent father, mother, and sister were carried away in a transport to their deaths. The ever present thought that he alone has lived, and why? Mr. A. became convinced that he had survived only to be able to tell the story of the extermination of European Jewry.

I became his English mouthpiece. Perhaps I have helped him. Perhaps I have told our people's history to those who would not have heard it otherwise.

Ironically, I grew up sheltered from the Holocaust. We all knew about it, but no one dared talk about it in the fifties and sixties. I knew that Hitler had slaughtered our European family. I knew that my great-grandparents and cousins had been lined up and shot in their small village. I knew that I was named after my grandmother's mother who had not wanted to travel to America. Her name was Frayde— "happiness"—which my parents translated into English as Joyce. But how can a child feel the presence of a family that died before she was born?

It wasn't until adulthood that I realized the shelter of our North American homes hid a silence too shocking to dispel. For more than twenty years after World War II no one talked. Were Jews ashamed we had been slaughtered? Did we think we hadn't fought back hard enough? Parents didn't tell their children much. Friends of mine grew up not knowing they'd had older brothers and sisters who had died in the gas chambers at Auschwitz. Instead, we grew up with all the accoutrements of middle-class normalcy. I grew up in a New York neighbourhood where children watched TV, did their homework, went to summer camp, competed for grades, and sported the latest fashions. We didn't talk about the silences in our homes. We didn't mention the grandparents who weren't there. We ignored the purple tattooed numbers the Nazis had branded on our Hebrew teachers' arms. But the silence was a charade. One day it would have to end.

When did the illusion burst? Probably in 1967 after the Six Day War in Israel. A high school student at the time, I hadn't given much thought to the Jewish homeland. But I remember my mother gazing at the cover of *Life Magazine* in June of that year. The photograph showed a Jewish soldier in uniform. Everyone was talking about it. Everyone was incredulous. The image of the Jew, the stereotype of the Jew, had changed overnight from victim to fighter, from fearful prey herded into a cattle car to triumphant soldier who embodied the new Jewish psychology of "never again."

Soon stories began to seep from survivors' hearts. Adult children and growing grandchildren encouraged family members to tell their histories. Some suvivors hesitated, resisting the painful onslaught of memories, but others responded to a growing demand from publishers, television producers, archives, and museums that the crippling silence end. Today there are Holocaust museums in major cities around the globe. Making the film *Schindler's List* inspired director Steven Spielberg to videotape thousands of survivors all over the world, enabling their stories to be preserved forever. Each year in April the Jewish world commemorates Holocaust victims with ceremonies. Soon the remaining survivors themselves will pass on, but their voices will not be forgotten.

Yet some people's stories can never be told. There is no one left to tell them. On the dresser in my bedroom there sits a black-and-white photograph. My great-grandmother, Frayde, and her husband, Chaim, are standing on the wooden balcony of their home. It is a summer day in the late 1930s. The couple look sad; perhaps they're uncomfortable being photographed. Beside them are their two adult children and two grandchildren. The adult children, Toba and Nathan, seem modern, at ease. The grandchildren are smiling mischievously: the little boy in his sailor suit and crisp white hat, the girl—no older than two—grasping the bar of the balcony.

What did the Nazis think as they shot these children against a wall in the town of Monastrikh, Poland?

There is no one left who can even tell me their names.

Joyce Rappaport
Montreal, Quebec

North American Jews now comprise almost half of the world's Jewish population and number twice those in the state of Israel. The history of Judaism in North America is long and distinguished and includes active involvement with the development of Quebec and Canada. Beginning with a handful of merchants arriving in Halifax in 1749, through the establishment of the first synagogue in Montreal (1777), to subsequent waves of immigration from Eastern and Central Europe, Canada has been home to generations of Jews, both religious and secular.

In the late 1990s the Jewish population of Canada totals about three hundred thousand. Predominantly an urban population, most of the country's Jews live in Toronto and Montreal. Nonetheless, Jews have also always lived in rural communities, in such diverse areas as Newfoundland and the Yukon. Although Jews have lived in Canada for centuries, the majority arrived in two major periods of immigration—the first two decades of the twentieth century and the post–World War II period. Jews in Canada have a strong federation that links their communities with the Jewish community in Israel. Jews in the larger cities also have an independent day-school system that provides education in both Jewish and secular studies.

As is true in the United States, Canadian Jews generally affiliate with one of four religious movements within Judaism: the Conservative movement, Orthodoxy, Reconstructionism, and the Reform movement. Each of these interprets Jewish law differently, with Orthodoxy at one end holding that history and secular changes have no bearing on strict interpretations of the law and with the Reform movement on the other end of the spectrum saying that Jewish ritual is an option in modern society. Conservative Judaism, which was founded in the late nineteenth century, combines tradition and change and occupies the middle position between Orthodoxy and Reform. Reconstructionist Judaism blends egalitarian and democratic thinking with tradional practices. Many Jews also consider themselves to be secular—identifying strongly with the historical and cultural aspects of the Jewish people while rejecting to greater or lesser degrees the area of ritual.

Issues that are of special concern to Jews in Canada (and throughout the world) include the role of women in ritual, the definition of who is a Jew (each movement has its own standards for conversion and for deciding whether Judaism is passed down through matrilineal or patrilineal patterns), intermarriage, Israel's survival, and the theme of the Holocaust.

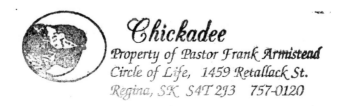

Chickadee
Property of Pastor Frank Armistead
Circle of Life, 1459 Retallack St.
Regina, SK S4T 2J3 757-0120

SHANNON'S SONG

As a Muslim I accept the Qur'an to be the very word of God, revealed to the Prophet Muhammad in the seventh century. It is in the words of the Qur'an that I find the themes that are important to me: love and mercy, peace, justice, and compassion. At this point in my life one verse in particular is most meaningful. (The translation from the Arabic original is my own.)

> *...And God has put between you Love and Mercy.*
> *Truly in this are Signs for those who reflect.*
>
> Qur'an 30:21

Many verses in the Qur'an speak of the "Signs of God," which are everywhere. Trying to understand or decipher these signs is one of the duties incumbent upon all Muslims. As I understand it, the verse speaks of the love and mercy that are found in human relationships, specifically, the relationship between married people (mentioned in the verse immediately prior). And the root or cause of human love and mercy is divine love and divine mercy, two of the attributes of God.

I did not truly begin to understand the many levels of meaning of this verse until I met my wife, Shannon L. Hamm. Shannon was born in Winnipeg and grew up in southern Manitoba a member of The United Church of Canada. To say that Shannon was the most amazing woman that I had met would be an understatement. She was so involved with the world; she loved to travel, talk, dance, and especially sing. While I remember her as a singer, she was also a first-rate thinker, the recipient of many academic awards, and a truly gifted teacher, whether working with university students, abused women, mentally disabled children, or head-injured adults. And she worked with all of these. Shannon and I were married on August 19, 1989. The service we designed included readings from both Christianity and Islam, including a longer passage from the Qur'an that contained the verse above.

Shannon challenged my world, the know-it-allness that only a twenty-three-year-old male can have. She taught me about peace and justice and the need to make a difference with our lives. Although she discovered her answers within a Christian framework, she helped me to find my own answers within a Muslim framework. This is important for me to say because terrible misunderstandings persist about Islam as a religion of violence and Muslims as a violent people, stereotypes which are as destructive for Islam as they are for any other world religion.

As I read the Qur'an, I discovered its overwhelming emphasis on the mercy and compassion of God: the idea that reconciliation and forgiveness are preferable to retribution, that mercy takes precedence over wrath. In addition to the Qur'an, Muslims have the life of the Prophet Muhammad as an example. In reading about his life, I repeatedly encountered images of love and compassion, ranging from everyday acts, like playing with his grandchildren, to acts of statesmanship in forgiving those who had persecuted him for the ethical monotheism he preached. And

I discovered countless examples in the Muslim tradition of people who practised mercy and justice, people such as Badshah Khan, who worked with Gandhi using non-violent resistance as a way to end colonial domination in South Asia.

I learned that these teachings of peace and justice were not foreign to Islam but an integral part of it. To me, this was the secret of interfaith dialogue—not that we seek to convert each other, but that we help one another find what is meaningful in our own traditions—that Shannon, as a Christian, could help me become a better Muslim.

Transformed by my experience with Shannon, I began to do interfaith work, largely, but not exclusively, with the United Church. The challenge to work towards a just society led me to join a number of groups, including the World Conference on Religion and Peace, the World Interfaith Education Association, and Science for Peace. Again I did all this within a Muslim framework, trying to follow the examples that I had been given from within my own tradition.

And then my world changed.

On July 7, 1992, Shannon died suddenly of a pulmonary embolism. I was twenty-six; hers was the first death of someone close to me, and I had no words for it, no models for my grief. At that point I did not stop believing, but I did not know what to believe. I could not reconcile the ideas of a loving and merciful and all-powerful God with a God that would let Shannon die. At her death Shannon was twenty-eight, the clinical manager of the Centre for Behavioural Rehabilitation, working with people with acquired brain injury. She was the classic example of a wonderful young woman doing important, ground-breaking work. And I could not imagine a God that would let her die, taking her away so quickly from such critical labours.

Of course, I have never been the same since. Shannon's death taught me many things, and in her death she continues to be one of my teachers. I remember old conversations in different ways, thankful for a teacher who left me with answers to questions I had not yet learned to ask. And while there has been none of the communication with Shannon that I have so desperately sought since her death, occasionally I am blessed with some sense that she is still here—that her song is still being sung in her own beautiful voice.

One of the times I heard this song was while offering prayers in the Lodge at the Dr. Jessie Saulteaux Resource Centre in Beausejour, Manitoba, in a gathering led by Stan McKay and Janet Silman. The Lodge that day held people from several traditions, and we all prayed together as well as offered our own prayers in our own languages. Another time was at a United Church service in Toronto. July 7, 1996, was the fourth anniversary of Shannon's death, and it happened to fall on a Sunday. I had no idea what to do with myself that day. For no conscious reason that I can recall, I decided to go to the church that Shannon sometimes attended in Toronto, Trinity–St. Paul's on Bloor Street. I had never been to a church by myself for no reason before. The minister, Joan Wyatt, was on holiday, and the service was conducted by Michael Cooke, Juliet Huntly, and Sarah Yoon. And everything about that service was connected to Shannon, as if it were her memorial service. We sang one of her favourite hymns, there was a reading from a book she loved, the importance of meaningful work was stressed, and we held hands and danced for the closing hymn. Of course, these people had no knowledge of Shannon, and I had never met any of them prior to that day's service. It was just one of those magical moments.

Despite such moments I have also come to understand that my faith, my Islam, does not bring me healing. Instead, it does something infinitely more powerful. It allows me to live broken. It allows me to understand something of the gift that is life. As a believer, I know that at some point, Shannon, God, and I will meet again. And I will be asked what I did with this life I was given, what difference I made with that life.

And I have been so incredibly fortunate to be given a life, and texts for how to live that life, and a teacher to help me read those texts, and many more teachers since that first, best teacher. In the fall of 1997 I returned to San Francisco, a city I had last visited five years before, only months after Shannon's death. Five years later an important change came over me. As I sat down to a meal with one of my teachers, professor Michel Desjardins of Wilfrid Laurier University, I realized just how many gifts I had been given. The question that I had been asking—"Why me?"—was still my question; its emphasis, however, was totally different. Instead of "Why me? Why am I so cursed? Why do I no longer have Shannon around?" now the question was "Why me? Why am I so fortunate to be given so many teachers and friends?"

What will I do with all that has been given to me? In my own poor way I too will try to sing Shannon's song. I turned to my favourite complete chapter of the Qur'an (chapter 93), "The Morning," and found solace:

> *By the morning.*
> *By the night when it is still.*
> *Your Lord has not forsaken you, nor is your Lord*
> *displeased*
> *And The Last will be better for you than The First*
> *And your Lord will give you so you will be content*
> *Did your Lord not find you an orphan and shelter*
> *you?*
> *And find you erring, and guide you?*
> *And find you needy, and enrich you?*
> *So do not treat the orphan harshly.*
> *Nor drive away the petitioner.*
> *And proclaim the bounty of your Lord.*

These words were first given to the Prophet Muhammad and through him, to all people, myself included. They are the words to Shannon's song. Help people. Work towards justice and mercy in this world. Proclaim the goodness of the Lord.

Let her song be sung.

Amir Hussain
Northridge, California

There is no accurate count of the number of Muslims in Canada. A reasonable number to suggest, based on immigration patterns, is about four hundred thousand. Most Canadian Muslims are immigrants, or the children of immigrants, and the largest group is of South Asian origin. Islam is a religion that encourages conversion, and there is a small but growing number of Canadian converts as well.

Although the majority of Muslim immigrants to Canada came or were born after the immigration reforms of the 1960s, there have been Muslim families in Canada for well over a hundred years. The first mosque was built in Edmonton in 1938. There are now mosques in most major cities, since most Canadian Muslims, like most Canadians, live in the country's large urban centres. Islamic organizations in Canada date from 1953 with the founding of the Federation of the Islamic Associations of the USA and Canada.

When describing their religious practices, Muslims will often speak of three dimensions: *Islam* (submission), *Iman* (faith), and *Ihsan* (doing what is beautiful). Islam, the name given to the tradition, is often described as activity, and Muslims refer to the "Five Pillars" as the fundamental activities of Islam. These consist of 1) The "Witness." This is the faith statement that "There is no God but God, and Muhammad is the Messenger of God." 2) Daily prayers. In the Sunni tradition of Islam Muslims are obliged to pray five daily prayers, with Friday being the day of communal prayer and the Friday noon prayer being the congregational prayer. 3) Alms or charity. A portion of one's wealth is given for charitable works. 4) Fasting. Muslims fast during the month of Ramadan. 5) Pilgrimage to Mecca. Once, if possible, Muslims should make the pilgrimage to Mecca.

Iman, or faith, refers to a deeper level of understanding. Muslims are required to have faith in God, God's angels, God's revealed books, God's messengers and prophets; in the Last Day; and in the justice of God. *Ihsan*, or "doing what is beautiful," refers to a deeper level still of intentionality—the idea of seeing God in reality and living and behaving with sincerity and a constant God-wariness.

The two major festivals in Sunni Islam are both referred to as *Eid*, the Arabic word for celebration. One *Eid* comes at the end of the month of fasting; the other comes during the month of pilgrimage and commemorates the sacrifice of Abraham. These holidays rotate throughout the Islamic calendar, which is lunar.

THE TAOIST WAY
AND THE VALUES OF LIFE

*Family and wealth cast off, they are not
your own possessions.*

Understanding Reality

*It is impossible to count the things our
parents have done for us.
Not even giving our life would be enough to
repay them.*

The Jade Emperor's Sutra of Filial Gratitude

Among my favourite stories from the Taoist tradition is that of
Immortal Lu Tung-Pun, one of the famous Eight Immortals of
Chinese folk religion, and his decision to leave aside the world of
politics and material success. Like many ambitious and talented
young men of his time Lu set out for the capital city to take the
Imperial Examinations that would qualify him for a life of wealth
and prestige in the Chinese civil service. On the way he stopped
at an inn, where a kindly, white-haired stranger offered him several
cups of warmed wine.

The wine put Lu to sleep, and he dreamed of rising to the
highest position in the Emperor's court, sitting at the Emperor's
right hand, and holding tremendous power. But soon this
superiority produced powerful enemies who conspired to disgrace

the young upstart. After only a short moment of glory Lu found himself banished to the ends of the empire, his closest family members dead or impoverished, all of his dreams having turned to dust.

Upon awakening from his stupor, Lu saw immediately the emptiness of his worldly ambitions and the superior strengths of the man who had granted him this vision. Lu asked to be taken on as a student of this enlightened teacher and henceforth devoted himself to the study of the Tao. After years of diligent practice Lu became an immortal who dedicated himself to helping the sick and the poor. He is also known as a synthesizer of the three great religions of China: Taoism, Buddhism, and Confucianism.

As a university professor, daughter, wife, mother, and student of the Tao, I often look to this story to remind myself of the emptiness of ambition and worldly attachments. And as the above lines from *Understanding Reality* suggest, attachment can include family as well as material wealth and social position. Yet the Taoist tradition, as I know it, does not advocate quietism and isolation from the world. It is said that the greatest sage lives in the city, working among and helping others.

It is also said in the Taoist tradition that when you are ready, the teacher will appear. And so it happened that my husband and I were introduced to Master Moy Lin-Shin while we were graduate students in Toronto. We began studying Taoist Tai Chi with Master Moy, and subsequently became members of Fung Loy Kok Institute of Taoism, an organization that follows the Chinese "three religions" tradition sometimes associated with Immortal Lu. When I met Master Moy, I was unaware of the depth of teachings he would open up to me. Over the years I have come to see that he helped me re-focus my life and ambitions in a manner not unlike that of Immortal Lu and his teacher.

Throughout the stages of life I have had ample occasion to assess my commitments to both job and family and to see these as part of, rather than in tension with, my own spiritual development. The task for me has been to find ways to follow my spiritual path within a late twentieth-century work and family life—to live fully and richly with students and colleagues, family and friends, without losing my spiritual direction. Over the years this struggle has meant letting go of the ambition to be either super-mom or at the top of my profession. I can remember several occasions when my teacher, Master Moy, reminded me that without taking care of myself, I would not have the "substance" to be of any real help to others. I have had to put aside the desire to give the ultimate birthday party or to nurture my daughter, students, or career at the expense of my health. Instead, I have tried to let my actions in every role be guided by wisdom and compassion, rather than by ego and desire.

The recent death of my seventy-six-year-old mother has given me a new occasion to reflect on what Taoist training has taught me about relating to others in a world that eventually demands the ultimate letting go that death represents. Sitting at my mother's bedside in her final days, trying to comfort her as she once comforted me, I felt her return these gestures with her own small signs that she felt my presence. I'm not sure who was doing the comforting, even then. But I thought often of the Confucian virtue of filial gratitude, and of how profound gratitude for all that my mother had given me throughout her life gave me a peaceful (if not entirely painless) way of letting her go.

One expression of this virtue, The Jade Emperor's Sutra of Filial Gratitude, graphically tells the story of a mother's sacrifices for her child. From the first, anxious desire to have a child, through the discomforts of pregnancy, nursing, childhood illnesses, and worries over a wild adolescence, the scripture depicts the mother willingly undertaking a life of hardships in order to raise her offspring. The mother (and father, though he is less present in this late eighteenth– or early nineteenth-century text) becomes a model of absolute selflessness in her role as caregiver, guardian, and guide. And the text reminds us that while we can never repay our parents for this debt, it should be in our nature to be grateful to them and to emulate their sacrifices in our own selfless giving to others.

I cannot fully explain why I found this gratitude so valuable on the occasion of my mother's death. Perhaps part of the reason lies in the recognition that though now physically absent, this person who meant so much to my life lives on—not just genetically, in her children and grandchildren, but in all the deeds that have shaped my life and the lives of others around her. Through her life she offered me a model of giving to family, church, and community that I now realize has guided my actions and will, I hope, serve as a model for my daughter and for generations to come.

Returning to the rather austere but beautiful Presbyterian church of my childhood for my mother's memorial service was also comforting. The scripture, the hymns, the organ music, and the faces of so many who had shepherded my brothers and myself through childhood helped temper feelings of sadness and loss with a sense of continued connection. Few in that congregation would have been aware that my own spiritual path had taken a different, yet not incompatible, direction. As I sat in my cushioned pew, I was in fact also preparing for the upcoming funeral of my Taoist teacher, Master Moy Lin-shin, who, in one of life's inexplicable coincidences, had died that very morning.

One thing that struck me during that time was how similar the teachings and practices of Christianity and Taoism are, even though their cultural contexts are so very different. I don't wish to blur differences, but both traditions do remind us that life on this earth is short, that we are here to help and serve others in whatever roles we may play, and that it is by our deeds, however great or small, that we will finally be known. Both Taoism and Christianity emphasize the importance of community, sharing spiritual values, and supporting each other through times of joy and sorrow. And both faiths regard the family as a centre of moral and spiritual development.

At my mother's memorial service I quoted a letter from her father, praising her for knowing "how to keep the price tags arranged on the values of life." Writing this essay, I see that recognizing the true values of life was also part of Immortal Lu's lesson. To both my mother and my teacher, Master Moy, I owe a debt I can never repay. I remain deeply grateful to both of them, especially for the ways they have helped me to see what is of value, to let go of what is not, and to let my life be guided by their fine examples.

Karen Laughlin
Tallahassee, Florida

One of the world's most ancient religions, Taoism is deeply woven into the fabric of China, where it has developed in dynamic relation to Chinese culture, folk religions, and the great traditions of Confucianism and Buddhism, which developed both alongside and within Taoism. The roots of Taoism are in China's prehistory: traces of ancient shamanistic rituals are still found in religious ceremonies, as shamanistic healing practices have been carried forward in the Taoist emphasis on cultivating health of both body (or life) and mind (or spirit). Taoism's impact on North America and around the world is strongly linked to the graceful Taoist art of T'ai Chi Ch'uan (Supreme Ultimate Movements).

A high point of Taoism's development came in the philosophical classics attributed to Lao Tzu, who lived in the sixth century BCE, and to Chuang Tzu, who lived some four hundred years later. From Lao Tzu comes the Tao Te Ching, one of the world's most translated books, with its emphasis on peacefully following the natural way of things and on living in harmony with both nature and our fellow beings. Lao Tzu and other Taoist sages understood the Tao as the source, or origin, of all creation, an undifferentiated wholeness that existed before heaven and earth. To follow the way of the Tao (Tao can also be translated as the Path, or the Way) is to return to this state of non-differentiation. Taoist mystics, sages, and practitioners have developed myriad techniques to aid in this process. Many of these revolve around physical exercises for developing optimum physical health while also focusing on compassion and taming the heart—letting go of desires and negative emotions to let the original spark of goodness residing in each of us shine brightly and direct our actions.

Formal organization of Taoism as a religion occurred in the second century CE, and included a hierarchy of priests, a monastic tradition, and formal religious ceremonies that recognized Lao Tzu as patriarch and as a manifestation of the Tao. Today there is a strong lay tradition in Taoism that often focuses on physical training methods such as T'ai Chi and meditation and a ceremonial tradition practised by clergy and lay people alike.

Taoist practices may be understood in terms of three "vehicles" for attaining enlightenment (or returning to the Origin). The first is a secular approach based on maintaining a morally upright lifestyle and doing good deeds; the second vehicle is to follow the traditional Taoist temple rituals and ceremonies; while the third vehicle may be described as engaging in the path known as "*xingming shangxiu*," or dual cultivation of body and mind.

Fung Loy Kok Institute of Taoism, which has branches in Canada, the USA, Hong Kong, Australia, and New Zealand, exemplifies the third vehicle. Its training methods are based on the belief that enlightenment, as conceived in the Taoist tradition, can be best attained by the joint cultivation of bodily health and spiritual values. Fung Loy Kok also exemplifies the "three religions" tradition of Taoism, bringing together teachings of Confucianism, Buddhism, and Taoism. Confucian propriety, Buddhist scriptures, and Taoist training methods are seen as united in the Tao. The stated mission of Fung Loy Kok, "To deliver all souls from suffering and to provide services to the living and the dead," reflects both a strong emphasis on compassion and a belief that the unified wisdom of these three traditions can best serve the modern world.

THE PEPAL TREE

Guru Gobind Singh, Tenth Master of the Sikhs, was travelling in the village of Soheva when he came across a cluster of jand trees. In the trunk of one of these trees was a sapling that he had first encountered during meditation. "Usually, the white saplings of the pepal tree do not grow in desert areas because they are very tender," the guru remarked. "But this small pepal tree will grow into a mighty tree and outgrow the jand," he prophesied. "That is the time when my Khalsa (those who live their values) will spread to the four corners of the world. Then the spirit of the order of the Khalsa, which I have enshrined under the command of the Creator, shall set up a world society which will last five thousand years. That divine society will enjoy peace and abundance."

It is said that the pepal has now begun to overgrow the jand tree.

God's will. Accept God's will. Understand God's will. Live in God's will. What does all this really mean? I have grappled with the issue time and again. Recently a profound experience gave me a taste of what this struggle does mean and of the freedom and deep contentment that are in store when I make God's will my spiritual default position.

Being a Sikh is my spiritual identity. I experience my soul as a Sikh. I feel life's experiences with my heart, as a woman. But the events which have had the most profound effect on me are those I have experienced as a yogi, beyond the polarities of time and space, beyond even my heart centre. My most profound experiences have been when my spirit has been challenged beyond what I have imagined, to the point of transformation. My mind can only grasp such experiences symbolically. Still, I am changed forever.

The Siri Guru Granth Sahib, in the form of a collection of sacred words, contains the essence of Sikh teachings. These serve as the Living Guru, or guide, to all Sikhs. The Guru is the eternal wisdom of God that reveals to us the interdependence of all that is. In its first words the Siri Guru Granth Sahib invokes God's qualities and provokes us with the notion of God's will:

> *All is the One Universal Creator God, whose Name is Truth, who is Creative Being Personified; with No Fear, No Hatred; the Image of the Undying; Beyond Birth; Self-Existent. By the Guru's Grace: Chant and Meditate! True in the Primal Beginning, True throughout the ages. True here and now. O Nanak, forever and ever true!*

Yes, I can accept that. But just as I start to feel comfortable, I come across the following line: "By thinking, He cannot be reduced to thought, even by thinking hundreds of thousands of times." Oh, so thinking won't liberate me. Well, what will?

By remaining silent, inner silence is not obtained,
even by remaining lovingly absorbed deep within. The
hunger of the hungry is not appeased even by piling up
loads of wordly goods. Hundreds of thousands of
clever tricks, but not even one of them will go along
with you in the end.

(So, I can't fake it either.)

So how can one become truthful? And how can the veil
of illusion be torn away? O Nanak, it is written that
you shall obey the Order of His Command, and walk
in the Way of His Will.

Oh dear, there goes that word—obey. "*Obey* his will." It sounds as if I am supposed to grin and bear it as I go through life. Well, I have been good at doing that. I have risen above terrible losses and failures and been victorious in many ways. And through it all I have maintained my love of God. I have a wonderful, blessed life. Is that accepting God's will? I suppose so, yet it seems so passive. What about *my* will? God gave me free will, right? And how do I know what God's will is, anyway? So goes a typical conversation between my mind and ego.

But God's merciful glance once more illuminated my soul, and I came to a deeper understanding of this dilemma in the midst of great tragedy.

Last year we lost the son of a very dear friend. This young man was only twenty-one years old, and his death was tragic. I officiated at his funeral, attended by thousands of people. The whole thing was very sad. It was a challenge for me to hold the space in a dignified manner, while honouring the terrible grief and confusion written on the faces of mourners, as they passed by his body to pay their last respects.

I had known this young man his entire life. He had had his ups and downs; he was an innocent soul with a difficult life. He would swing back and forth between wanting to dedicate himself to higher ideals and being a party animal. Unable to reconcile these two passions, he went to the extreme in both directions. I was always there for him, and he looked to me for hope and, I suppose, forgiveness. I did my best to encourage him and let him know of God's love.

Several weeks passed after his death. His father took the son's ashes to India to perform special prayers with a holy man to whom the youth had been close and to perform the seventy-two hour *akhand paath* (continuous reading of the Siri Guru Granth Sahib's 1,473 pages). The ceremony was to be performed at a gurdwara, where this holy man would officiate.

I was away from home, resting for a few days in Whistler. One night I had a dream. I dreamt that the young man came to me and asked for my help. Strangely, he appeared as a two-year-old. Feeling his innocence and purity, I answered lovingly, "Of course, I will help you." The next thing I knew, I awoke and felt as if the crown centre at the top of my head—what Sikhs call the "Tenth Gate"— was strained. Actually, it is hard to explain exactly what I felt.

According to yogic anatomy we are made up of ten bodies, of which the physical body is only one. Our soul is also considered one of these bodies. At the time of death the soul is captured by the subtle body when leaving the physical plane after the pranic body, or life force, collapses.

What I felt that night was as if my subtle body were being used by God to help the soul of the young man through its transition. It is important to understand that this helping was in no way personal. It was not *me* doing it, with my big ego. (Remember, I had to be asleep for this surrender to take place.) What was mine, though, was the act of surrender. Out of pure love for this young man's soul, I had consented in the dream to help him. My saying, "Of course, I will help you" was all God needed. God's plan for that young man was perfect. All I had to do was give my love and step out of the way.

The next morning I called the young man's family only to discover that just at the time my dream was occurring, the *akhand paath* was ending, and the last prayer was being offered.

I realized at that moment what it means to be in God's will.

The realm of the subtle body is one of pure love. Its role is to expand and bless, to step out of the way in order to let God's magnificent wisdom manifest and carry us unto glory. But we are not powerless bystanders the way I used to think, just accepting,

accepting. Somehow, we are an integral part of this interaction. Our surrender to the divine plan, which is fuelled by love, unleashes this power. Somehow, the subtle body surrenders in service to God's will, and this surrender succeeds in direct proportion to how much we step out of the way—a task beyond cleverness, manipulation, or emotion. Think of it: Jesus' subtle body is still acting on us, as is Guru Nanak's, Guru Ram Das', and those of all God's great servants. The subtle body never dies.

And what is God's will, the divine plan? That each soul merge in divine love.

The rest of our strain and our pain, our struggle, our insecurity is our resistance. Resistance is simply the fear we have of adding our will to God's. We are always in the process of either resisting or surrendering to God's will. In that surrender to the divine we unleash the infinite glory of God, what Sikhs call *Sahej*, the easy acceptance of our own radiance, because it is God's radiance shining forth from us. And the experience of ecstasy when this great "creative wisdom" is experienced is what Sikhs call *Wahe Guru*.

The essence of the Sikh path is the marvellous balance between living one's life in a saintly way and as a spiritual warrior, between surrender and responsibility. The ability to remain universal and simultaneously maintain an underlying commitment to one's own path has not yet been fully realized, yet I have always felt that these seeds will flower in the coming times. Just like the pepal tree over which Guru Gobind Singh prophesied, the Khalsa spirit of each faith has been quietly evolving, the roots growing deeper and stronger, steadily creating a structure for leadership and inspiration. Like the pepal tree the flowering of the Khalsa of all faiths is inevitable, guided by destiny. And the flowers of that pepal tree are found in people all over the world—people who are giving hope, offering techniques to handle the stresses of the times, reaching out to one another. It is the fragrance of these flowers that contributes to the overpowering of the fear and separateness afflicting society. It is the radiance and warmth of these individuals throughout the world who are answering the great calling forth to live in love.

*Through God's Will come all created beings, though
God's Will can never be defined....All beings live
under the Will of God; None lives outside God's Will.
O Nanak, if one were to see the working of God's Will,
that one would not be filled with foolish pride.*

Guru Granth Sahib, pg. 1.

Okay, I get it.

Guru Raj Kaur Khalsa
Vancouver, British Columbia

The word Sikh is Punjabi for learner or disciple; Sikhism arose
during Hindu–Muslim conflicts in the Punjab region of North India
in the fifteenth century. Scholars regard Sikhism either as a reform
movement of Hinduism or as a blend of Hinduism and Islam.
Sikhs, however, reject these views and emphasize instead the divine
revelation received by their founder, Guru Nanak (d. 1539). Nanak's
central teaching was on the nature and worship of God: Sat Nam
(the True Name God or True One) is at once a personal god,
whose home is the human heart, and the infinite, immortal,
omniscient creator.

The tenets of the Sikh way of life evolved over the lifetimes of
ten successive visionaries called gurus. In 1699 Guru Gobind Singh,
the Tenth Master, instituted the Khalsa—those totally committed
to the Sikh way of life—and established a code of discipline. This
code, based on purity and simplicity, now includes abstention
from hair-cutting, tobacco, drugs, meat, and alcohol. The tying of
the turban over the spiritual crown is also a distinguishing
characteristic. Places of worship are called gurdwaras, meaning
"gate to the Guru, the Giver of Light." The Guru Granth Sahib is
the embodiment of the sacred words originally recited by the ten
visionaries and by enlightened people of other faiths when in a
state of ecstasy and is considered to be the Living Guru or guide
for Sikhs for all time.

Sikh dharma teaches the oneness of God, selfless service, unity
of all people, truthful living, and meditation. Sikhs consider people
of all races, religions, and gender to be equal. Ascetic renunciation
is de-emphasized. Discerning and following the will of God in

everyday life are stressed instead. God is regarded as being in all persons, accessible through prayer and meditation rather than through intermediaries or elaborate ritual observance.

In 1969 a man known as Yogi Bhajan arrived in the United States to teach yoga and Sikh technology. What he found was a generation of people searching for the simplicity and purity of a spiritually based society. Yogi Bhajan was the inspiration for many non-Indians worldwide who have since become Sikhs.

Sikhs now live the world over. In India they number several million, and the largest diaspora concentration is in the UK. In 1997 the Sikh community in Canada celebrated its one hundredth anniversary and in April, 1999, the three hundredth anniversary of the Khalsa. Up until the first half of the twentieth century there were relatively few Canadian Sikhs; many cut their hair or beards and removed their turbans in an effort to assimilate. Over the last thirty years, however, there has been a return to the essential values of the faith, as Sikhs have put down roots and grown confident of their identity in the North American context. This shift has made Sikhs more visible in Canadian society. The past three decades have also seen the universalization of the faith realized, as people of all nationalities embrace the Sikh way of life.

THE PARSIS AND
THEIR SACRED FIRE

Over forty years ago just before my husband, my fourteen-month-old son, and I were to leave for Canada, I went to Udvada, a small sleepy village north of Bombay, to pray at the oldest *atash behram* (fire temple) of the Zoroastrian faith.

I was excited at the idea of making a home for my family in one of the loveliest, most secure parts of the world, but at the same time I felt apprehensive as the time of departure neared, full of doubt and a little sad. After all, I was leaving my family, all my friends, and the country I loved so much. Had my husband and I made the right decision to leave everything behind and venture so far away?

It was in this frame of mind that I entered the *atash behram*. After the obligatory washing of hands and a short prayer I entered a large dark room where the worshippers were either seated or standing in prayer. Our fire temples are simple. Except for a few symbolic sculptures on the exterior the temple is markedly bare, almost austere; there are no religious paintings or statues in the interior. The prayer room has rich Persian carpets and is so designed that the worshipper's total attention is focused on the sacred fire that blazes in a huge silver urn standing in the inner sanctum.

As I stood there gazing at the *Iran Shah*, our most ancient and sacred fire, I thought of the generations of Parsis who had suffered and sacrificed for their faith and of the millions over the centuries who must have communicated their joys and sorrows before the Holy Fire—the symbol of Ahura Mazda, God himself, and of our inner divine spirit.

After a while I underwent a remarkable experience: peace and calm descended on my troubled spirit; my cares vanished. I felt all would be well, and I returned from Udvada reassured and refreshed.

On my way back to Bombay I reflected that although I had some regrets leaving India, I was doing so of my own free will under conditions of security and peace and could always return to my homeland. How different was the situation of my ancestors who fled from Iran over a thousand years ago in dangerous times, knowing that they could never return to their homeland. Theirs is a story of high adventure, unflinching devotion to their faith, suffering and loss, and finally, triumph over great odds.

After the fall of the Persian Empire in 651 CE most Zoroastrians took refuge in remote, inhospitable parts of the country, where they thought they would be safe from ferocious Arab onslaughts. The descendants of some of these Zoroastrians continued to live in Iran, suffering oppression and great hardships over the centuries; many thousands still live there today. Others fled in diverse directions, to China, Central Asia, Eastern Europe, and Northern India, and over time were assimilated by local populations. Somehow, of all those who had left Iran, we Parsis managed to survive with our ethnicity and our religion intact. Was this an accident? Did we have a special role to fulfill? I wondered.

There is no documented history of our arrival in India or of the centuries we have lived there. Fragmentary accounts exist here and there in stories and ballads, and there are passing references in the historical record of the Hindus and in reports by travellers. One of the main sources of knowledge about our ancestral history is the *Qissa* (tale) *of Sanjan*, a versified account based on oral tradition, composed by a priest Dastur Behman Kaikobad, in 1600. The *Qissa* may be understood as our founding myth, or sacred story, regarding the origins of the Parsi diaspora community in India:

It appears that in the violence and chaos that followed after 651, when thousands were forced to convert to Islam, when fire temples were destroyed and wealth looted, our ancestors took refuge in the mountains of Khorasan in northeastern Iran, a region still under Zoroastrian control. Here the devotees survived for a hundred years until forced to flee again. The faithful then trekked across the barren plateau regions and deserts to arrive at the port of Hormuzd on the south coast, where they lived for another fifteen years.

Threatened by the spread of Islam, realizing that they could no longer continue as Zoroastrians in the land of their birth, and believing that safety lay in a sea route to India, they left in seven large junks to find a new homeland. The refugees landed in Diu, a small island south of the great Gujarat Peninsula, bringing with them the *alat*, sacred live embers from an old fire temple in Khorasan.

Once again, this home was not fated to be permanent. It was too exposed to storms and to the Arabs who had taken command of the sea routes. An old *dastur* (priest), well versed in astrology, advised the faithful to leave. So after nineteen years they left once again, sailing south to the mainland of India. On the way the sojourners met with fierce storms, and they prayed and vowed that should they land safely, they would build a fire temple as soon as possible and there consecrate the holy fire from the embers they had kept alive all this time.

Finally, around 937 CE a crowd of hungry, desperate men, women, and children landed in leaky boats at a village 145 kilometres north of the present city of Mumbai (Bombay). Summoned to the court of the local ruler, Jadi Ranah, the Zoroastrians' *dastur* came, carrying a small urn with the holy fire.

He explained that they were refugees from Iran in search of a new homeland where they could live in peace and practise their faith. Jadi Ranah told the newcomers they would be welcome in his kingdom, provided they accepted his terms: the relinquishing of all arms, adoption of the local language as the means of communication, acceptance of the sari as the women's apparel, adherence to certain local customs, and submission of a written account explaining the newcomers' faith.

The refugees readily agreed to these terms, and the generous ruler promised them vacant land where the weary travellers could settle. When asked what they would do for their adopted land, the wise *dastur* requested that a bowl of milk be brought. He then added sugar to the liquid and returned it, remarking that the sugar could not be seen but the milk was sweeter for it. The court understood the symbolic gesture and applauded. The Zoroastrians then prostrated themselves before the ruler and swore that they would be friends to all Hindustan.

This civilized encounter marked the beginning of our cordial relationship with the people of India. Our ancestors settled on the land they were given and named their new home, Sanjan, after a city in Khorasan where many of them had lived. Because most of the people had originally come from Pars, a province of the old Persian empire, they called themselves Parsis. After a time the magnanimous ruler gave them more land and all the material with which to build their fire temple. The devotees did so, afterwhich they set aflame the live embers, consecrated the Holy Fire, and named it *Iran Shah*, thus designating for all times the place of origin, in memory of their homeland, where Zoroastrianism was once the supreme religion. They also prepared Confessions of their Faith and Practices, a document written in Sanskrit, in which they not only explained their religion, but took the trouble to point out its similiarities to Hinduism.

Over the years more refugees arrived, and the Parsis spread to the surrounding towns and villages of Gujarat. Soon the industrious settlers established themselves in various vocations and prospered. Tragedy and loss, however, still haunted them. As Islam made inroads into India in the twelfth and thirteenth centuries, Zoroastrians were massacred at Variav and Cambay, decimating their already small numbers. The final disaster took place at the end of the fourteenth century, when Sanjan was attacked. Around 1400 some Parsis volunteered to fight and die under their leader Ardeshir. The others left with women and children for the rugged hills of Bahrot, taking with them once again the embers of the sacred fire. Here survivors lived for twelve years.

Early in the sixteenth century there was yet another attempt at forced conversion when the Portuguese governer of Thana demanded that Parsis accept Roman Catholicism or face death. The Parsis begged the governor that they be given four days in which to celebrate their religious festivals. Granted this request, the people organized massive banquets to which all the Portuguese were invited. Drink flowed freely, and in the midst of all the merrymaking, the Parsis stole away from Thana to safety.

Most of the Parsis continued to be farmers and craftsmen in the towns and villages of Gujarat, but a few ventured further afield. In 1578 the great Moghul emperor, Akbar, deeply interested in all the religions in his realm, summoned the Parsi leaders to a conference at the capital. Dastur Meherji Rana, accompanied by two other priests, arrived at Akbar's court and, it is said, made a great impression. Zoroastrian scriptures, already translated into Sanskrit, were now also translated into Persian. Over time more Parsis arrived at the courts of the Moghuls and served in various capacities. Many went to Surat, where Europeans had established trading outposts. Not burdened by caste restrictions in Surat, Parsis were able to mix freely with the Europeans. Many Parsis made their fortunes as middle men, as bankers, and in administrative positions for trading companies. The contact between Parsis and Europeans also marked the beginning of Western interest in Zoroastrianism; gradually, scriptures were translated into European languages, and scholarly works published.

In 1668 the East India Company acquired a number of small villages and islands which would become the future city of Bombay. Soon Parsis began arriving as well. After a time as the area became a centre of commerce and industry, Parsis migrated to Bombay in large numbers. By the end of the nineteenth century most Parsis had left their homes and rural lifestyle to build new lives for themselves in the bustling city. Eventually, in 1742 after many vicissitudes the holy *Iran Shah* came to rest in Udvada—a small village near Bombay. And there the sacred fire blazes today.

The period between 1850 and 1950 marked the zenith of Parsi wealth and influence. Parsis became great captains of industry; others excelled in commerce and trade initiatives with China and East Africa. Parsis excelled also in the professions, in the arts and sciences, and were great philanthropists. Two outstanding leaders for India's independence prior to Mahatma Gandhi were Sir Dadabhoy Navroji and Madame Cama.

Centuries ago the people of India had befriended the Parsis and given them life and hope. In turn Parsis enriched their adopted country and proved they were true sons and daughters of India. Today fewer than a hundred thousand Parsis are scattered around the globe. Although the majority still live in India, mainly in Bombay, there are thousands in the UK and North America and a few thousand in Australia and New Zealand. Now after centuries of separation from each other the Parsis and recent Zoroastrian emigrants from Iran have again come together in the Western world.

Sociological and demographic studies predict that given intermarriage, increased assimilation into Western culture, and the growing poverty in India and Iran, we Zoroastrians—many of whom prefer to be known by the alternative Iranian name, Zarathustis—will cease to exist as a people by the middle of the next century. I, however, feel otherwise. As long as the Sacred Fire burns at Udvada, and the sacred flame of the teachings of Zarathustra are kept alive in our minds and hearts, we will survive and make a positive contribution wherever we live.

> I prayed before the mystic fire
> I prayed and gazed anon;
> The flames they switched and leaped
> and danced
> And soon, as though in a golden trance,
> The flames and I were one.
> Gone were the sorrows of yesteryears,
> Gone were the petty crippling fears;

A radiant stillness enveloped my being,
A warmth and peace beyond all reckoning.
I saw the others deep in prayer,
Their faces radiant in the ruddy glow,
And in the darkening gloom
Of that inner sacred room
I knew why, through the ages, Man
Before the fire had bowed in prayer.

Soonoo Engineer
Vancouver, British Columbia

Zoroastrianism, once the imperial religion of ancient Iran, lost its status and rapidly dwindled in numbers of believers after the rise of Islam and conquest by the Arabs (651 CE). Despite much persecution and hardship a small number of Zoroastrians retained their faith. Fortunately, the largest diaspora community, which settled in the hospitable environment of India, managed to thrive. These constitute the majority of Zoroastrians, whose total population worldwide numbers around a hundred thousand.

Zoroastrianism owes its origins to the teaching of Zarathustra, who lived and taught in the North East Plateau of Iran around 1500–1400 BCE. The core of Zarathustra's teachings is embodied in the Gathas, five "songs" attributed to Zarathustra himself. He taught the worship of Ahura Mazda, one divine cosmic creative power which underlies and animates all creation. Humans are endowed with the divine spirit and are asked to realize our oneness with Ahura Mazda by following the precepts of Good Thoughts, Good Words, and Good Deeds, by struggling against evil and serving the needy. Zarathustra laid great emphasis on freedom of choice and personal responsibility. He preached that there was an afterlife, but its state was strictly determined by one's thoughts and actions while on earth, and he optimistically predicted the eventual spiritual rejuvenation of humankind.

Basic tenets of the faith also include respect for nature and upholding the equality of all peoples. As members of a minority religion Zarathustis, as they now prefer to be called, are adept at living in diaspora and respecting diverse customs and beliefs. Zarathustis do not proselytize, but interfaith dialogue plays an important role in extending awareness of this ancient tradition to others.

Zarathustis began settling in North America in the fifties and sixties. Today some fifteen thousand prosper in a variety of businesses and professions, enriching local communities through educational and cultural contributions and enterprising spirit. Currently there are eight temples in North America and over twenty associations.

"I'VE GOT SHOES, YOU'VE GOT SHOES":

Journeying to Freedom

So powerful is the light of unity that it can illuminate the whole earth....

It is incumbent upon all the peoples of the world to reconcile their differences and, with perfect unity and peace, abide beneath the shadow of the Tree of His care and loving-kindness.

Baha'u'llah

The journey began with Abraham. Not the Abraham you read about in the Bible or the Qur'an. No! This was Abraham whose mother was brought from Africa to the United States as a slave in the mid-1800s. No one remembers her name, but her story is still remembered.

The mother of Abraham taught him that all people were created by God, and she believed that they should all be free. She really believed that God wanted everyone to live together as one family. And she believed that this would one day happen in the world. She talked a lot about heaven, a place where everyone, no matter what their colour, could be free. She and the other slaves used to sing, "I've got shoes, you've got shoes, all God's chillun got shoes, and when we get to heaven, gonna put on our shoes and gonna walk all over God's heaven." Slave owners thought the refrains were about life after death, but the slaves were actually singing about Canada, the heaven they'd heard about, where they could live as free people—if they could only manage to escape.

Abraham's mother knew that she would never get to Canada, but she wanted her son to escape slavery. And he did, via the underground railroad, all the way to Ontario.

In the mid-1850s Abraham married a Mohawk girl named Marie, and they begat George. The story of Abraham's journey and his dream of freedom for "all God's chillun" was passed on. George married Martha, the daughter of Thomas, an American freed slave, and Hattie, a Cherokee. George and Martha begat Myrtle, and the story of the journey continued. Myrtle married Elvin. He was born in Montreal and was the son of Lemuel and Emily, who came to Canada from Barbados in the early part of this century. Then Myrtle and Elvin begat me, Shirlee.

I was told the story by my mother, Myrtle, and it was the fuel that started the fire burning within me—the yearning to continue my great-grandfather's journey to the heaven of freedom and equality for "all God's chillun." Deep in my soul I knew this was no mere dream. I always believed that the oneness of humankind would some day be a reality. But how could this be accomplished? There is so much hatred in the world. How can we learn to love one another? I knew by reading the Bible and listening to sermons that if we followed the words of Jesus, we could have peace and unity. I also knew that Buddha, Muhammad, and Krishna had all talked about peace and unity.

Yet the way the world was going, the idea seemed impossible. I thought and prayed about this for years, "Oh God! Show me the answers. Help me to understand." Then a remarkable thing happened. One day I was expressing my feeling to a friend, and he started talking to me about the Baha'i faith. He talked about the principles: the oneness of humankind, the equality of the races and of men and women, and the oneness of religion, that all religions come from God. My friend then went on to explain how Baha'u'llah, founder of the Baha'i faith, teaches that there is need for a universal language and basic education. I read some of the many prayers and writings of Baha'u'llah, and they spoke immediately to my heart and soul.

I was raised in a black Baptist church in Toronto, and many of the men in my family were clergy. When I learned to pray, it was mostly if I really wanted something or to heal somebody. The Baha'i concept of obligatory prayer was new to me; I found the idea of addressing God upon waking, before sleep, and at midday comforting. The Baha'i prayer book contains prayers written by Baha'u'llah, the manifestation of God for today. These prayers are for specific situations and for spiritual qualities. The only such prayer I'd ever known like this was the Lord's Prayer, left to us by Jesus, and this prayer had been a guide throughout my life. Suddenly, here was a goldmine of prayers praising God, more powerful than my own spontaneous prayers because they were the words of a representative of God. I still use the Lord's Prayer, but I also use Baha'i prayers.

My mother had told me that Abraham had to come through "many trials, toils, and snares" during his escape. Although there were welcoming people waiting for him, it must have taken a while for him to realize that he had arrived safely. When I found Baha'u'llah, I knew I had come to the end, or should I say the beginning, of my spiritual journey. This was the vision that Abraham's mother had seen so long ago. Then when I met members of the Baha'i community, I knew that I had come home, and in 1964 I became a Baha'i.

That happened in Bermuda. I must admit that, at first, it seemed too good to be true. After all, it was easy to talk about unity in diversity when they didn't really have diversity in that particular community, for at that time all the Baha'is in Bermuda save one were black. Would I feel as loved and welcomed in a Baha'i community that was more mixed?

In 1972 I returned to Canada and met the Baha'is here. I will never forget the joy and warmth with which I was, and am still, enveloped by my Baha'i family. We are of many races and of many national and cultural origins, but we know we are one family.

Yes! It is possible for people of every background to live together in harmony. The variety of races and cultures is what makes us more beautiful. The Baha'i writings describe the different races as being like "the flowers of one garden" and "the waves of the sea." There are millions of Baha'is around the world who believe this and who are praying and working to help others realize this as well. When this vision of unity is finally realized, we will all escape the slavery of prejudice. Then we can all sing "All God's chillun got shoes, and when we get to Heaven, gonna put on our shoes and gonna walk all over God's heaven." And this world will be as promised—the kingdom of God on earth. Heaven.

Shirlee Smith
Mississauga, Ontario

Baha'u'llah, founder of the Baha'i faith,was a Persian nobleman from Tehran who surrendered a privileged existence for a life of persecution and deprivation. He died in exile in 1892, having been imprisoned for progressive religious teachings that focused on the essential unity of humankind. Baha'u'llah taught that there is only one God, one human race, and that all religions reveal aspects of God's will and purpose for humanity. The time had come, he announced, for people to unite in a just and peaceful global society. To that end, he stressed universal education, the equality of men and women, the harmony of science and religion, and the abolition of prejudice. Baha'u'llah also foresaw this age in history as a time when peace and justice would be established throughout the world.

Six million people worldwide call themselves Baha'is; twenty-five thousand of these live in Canada in more than fifteen hundred localities and in every province and territory. The Canadian community dates from 1898, when the first Baha'i family moved to London, Ontario, and in 1902 a Baha'i group was organized in Montreal. By 1948 there were enough communities to elect a national governing body, the National Spiritual Assembly of the Baha'is in Canada, with headquarters in Thornhill, Ontario. In 1949 an act of Parliament incorporated the National Spiritual Assembly; Baha'i marriage is authorized under provincial law in every province.

In keeping with the vision of the faith as promoting world citizenship, Bahai's regard themselves as members of one human family and as servants of their country's best interests. The Baha'i Community of Canada collaborates actively with the Canadian International Development Agency (CIDA) and with national and provincial organizations that work toward eliminating prejudice; promoting racial unity; and supporting the advancement of women, the rights of children, and environmental protection. Wherever they live, Baha'is serve their fellow citizens and worship God through their labours, their prayers, and their love for humankind.

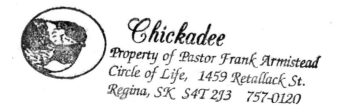

SPIRIT DANCE

I was ten when my mother was possessed by a stranger God. First, she made the decision to hold a Shango dance at our home. Two months after she left the Catholic church to become a Spiritual Baptist.

For three generations our family had served the God of the Catholic Church, faithfully and diligently, under the strict stewardship of my maternal great-grandmother, Gran-Gran. In this respect, my family's spiritual life had flowed along smoothly and undisturbed. My mother's unprecedented gesture was about to turn the tide.

In our family Gran-Gran was the undisputed queen, and in our village she was held in high regard. Like my mother Gran-Gran had also given birth to nine children. And she looked after successive generations of children as well, counting each like the rosary beads she swirled through her fingers. She never questioned her duty; this was the life she had created, and it gave her great satisfaction. As far as she was concerned, the Catholic God had protected her and taken care of her family's needs. Her faith was a matter of habit, pride, and social standing—a lifestyle my mother was now threatening with public embarassment.

The first day of the three-day event dawned sunny and beautiful, but dread lay heavy in my heart. For four weeks events at our house had built to an impending climax. For weeks the adults had whispered and grumbled. I felt their tension like a razor-sharp doom, the shadows gathering like clouds before a hurricane. Behind the agonized glances lay a secret I had yet to understand. I sensed it was a matter of survival.

I had heard about Shango dance before—a strange secretive practice that my slave ancestors had performed to preserve their beliefs and identity. I had heard about Voodoo and Obeah—it all amounted to devil worship, I'd been told. What I hadn't been told was the truth about African culture or about the miseries of slavery and the colonizers' fear and ignorance that kept our sacred traditions suppressed in the shadow areas of our culture.

Hearing outsiders' accounts of my family's predicament, I marvelled at my mother's courage. She shopped through it all, oblivious to the ripples her actions were creating. She cleaned, baked, and cooked, preparing a veritable feast for the occasion. All she would say in response to my questions was that we were in for a big surprise.

My heart ached for my father, bravely concealing his grief. He drank with the locals and told jokes and made light-hearted banter to keep spirits up. He was happy when he drank. Or so I thought.

On the day of the celebration I watched the throng of men, women, and children arriving at our house. My father had built a tarpaulin-covered tent in our backyard, and by evening it was filled with spectators.

I watched the activities unfold from a window overlooking the yard. Men arrived carrying drums and other African musical instruments. The women came dressed in white or red attire, according to rank. Most were barefoot, as a sign of respect, having removed their shoes before stepping on our soil. Later my mother explained that this was because our home was now a sanctuary for them, so they were stepping on holy ground.

For most of the day, three of the women in white huddled in private with my parents. One in particular—a scary-looking, coal-black woman who I later discovered was the mother superior—seemed to be running the show. She rarely smiled, but every now and then her sharp eyes fell on me like a touch of hot coal. Men and women, both, awaited her every word and obeyed her every wish with reverence and good humour.

The other women in white prepared what appeared to be an altar on a table inside the tent, covering the table with a clean white cloth, then placing a smooth washed stone at each corner. A chalice of water was set on a tray in the middle of the altar and surrounded with eight glasses of clean fresh water. The women decorated the altar with flowers, fruits, food, and family memorabilia. A calabash with kola nut was placed on the altar, and a candle was lit and placed beside it. Various other articles were also brought in and taken out over the course of the ceremony.

The women dressed in red took over running the house and the function; they cooked, served, cleaned, and engaged in light-hearted woman talk until evening.

At 6 PM sharp the ceremony began. It was a still evening; the island air was cool and clear. The mother superior, who had conferred with my mother for most of the day, now entered the ring. A hush fell on the crowd as she took a wide-legged stance in the middle of the circle. Hands on hips she stood for what seemed like eternity, still as a stone. Not so much as an eyelid flickered. Only her eyes moved, swimming in their sockets with bold confidence, as wise and alert as a snake's. She was a queen, resplendent in full regalia, from the sacred beads and rattles and white headdress mounting high above her head to the long white dress that fell around her full-figured body. Finally, she moved her head, slowly, surveying every inch of the crowd.

"Dis evening," she began, in a thick Grenadan country dialect, "an' for de next two days, you all goin' see someting good an' great an' beautiful. But hear dis you all. Dis is no place for the weak and the timid, cause we goin' to go back to Africa. An' de ride is goin' to be rough an' bumpy. We goin' to uplift the spirit an' touch de soul. We goin' to go back to dem long-bygone-freedom-days, an' be real good Africans again."

This was just the kind of talk Gran-Gran abhorred. To her mind, Afro-centric practices were "country folk ways," not to be taken seriously.

The woman in the circle began to talk about the seven African Spirits, deities with odd, unusual names like Elegba, the divine trickster, the smart talker. All ceremonies, she said, begin and end with Elegba, chief of divine forces, the spirit that slips in and out of our lives, bringing chaos or peace. Then there is Obatala, supreme creator of the Yoruba people. Obatala shapes the baby in its mother's womb and has jurisdiction over all human affairs. Obatala is the most benevolent, the most wise, and the most powerful judge and keeper of peace. Obatala, the woman said, is "all powerful, all forgiving, all vengeful, all brilliant, all retarded, all perfect, all deformed. All power belongs to Obatala. All respect is due Obatala."

She spoke about a beautiful goddess named Yemaya, the womb of creation. Yemaya is the mother of dreams, secrets, mysteries. She is the legendary mermaid who rules over all the great waters, the sea and rivers, the waters of the womb. Yemaya is the ruler of women's affairs, mother of productivity, ruler of the house, nurturer of children, and controller of the moon and women's cycles.

The regal figure in the circle kept on talking, conjuring images of the spirits as she spoke. There was Oya-Yana, the queen of the wind and sudden changes, who wields power over hurricanes, earthquakes, and natural disasters; and Oshun, "the daughter of the mountain," the African Venus, full of beauty, love, and sensuality. The woman told us of Ogun, the strong man who carries the world on his shoulders. Ogun is the great builder of the world and everything in it. He is the wild man of the woods, the controller of trade and commerce, the father of technology. But Shango, she said, was the androgynous spirit of humankind, the supreme dance between male and female, the warmth of the flame and the sacred fires—the spark of the human spirit. Shango is the child of Obatala, the adopted child of Yemaya, the child offered in sacrifice.

On and on the woman talked, spinning tale upon tale. When she finished, she opened her mouth, flicked out her tongue, threw her arms wide, and spun around three times, scraping her foot into the dirt floor. Suddenly, her hands flung to her head, and without warning a voice rose from her chest in the most plaintive and piercing wail I have ever heard. It flowed painlessly, permeating the crowd and all the universe. An electric shock shot through my spine and rippled through the crowd like a violent shudder.

No sooner had this command been given than three white doves were let loose. The first drum beat sounded, hitting like a blast of cold air. I had never felt anything so powerful; it made my heart spasm. Perception changed. The room lost its shape and dimensions. Trees were stilled, night creatures silenced. The women began to chant praises to Elegba, dancing to the drum. The crowd looked on spellbound.

I saw my mother walk into the circle, escorted by two women. Silent tears rolled down her cheeks, yet she looked peaceful. My father followed, escorted by two men. The women danced and prayed around the couple standing in the circle. My father looked dazed and disoriented. I watched, transfixed. I had seen my parents cry, but these were tears from some strange place I had never seen before.

The scary woman approached and shook my father's hand with strangely exaggerated spinning movements. With every shake and spin he would tremble and stumble as if about to fall; two helpers rushed to his side. My mother seemed more in control, and she responded to the greeting by imitating the woman's every movement. When the greeting was over, the helpers took my father by the hand and led him towards three drums to the right of the altar. The helpers each took possession of a drum, and my father followed their lead without protest. He sat down, placed the drum between his knees, rubbed his hands nervously on his thighs, then began to play. In the middle of the circle my mother danced alone.

She was a slight, beautiful woman of thirty. Her soft brown skin stretched smooth and firm across the surface of her body like a well-fitted brown quilt. Her crowning glory was a full head of thick black hair, which she wore tightly braided in a bun. But her most captivating feature was her eyes, dark and mysterious, trying to communicate the love and the hate, the pain and the courage that her life had been.

The music soared to a rich crescendo. I saw my mother trembling violently as she yielded to a being more powerful than herself. She became a being that felt deeply, one that loved and hated deeply, one that was completely free to express itself. She moved as if suddenly swept into orbit, as if intoxicated, as if she would explode.

All around the twilight dimmed. The latticework shadows faded. The darkness grew desolate, and the sounds of barking dogs faded into an intense background hum in the still, tropical night. I had never heard or seen anything so beautiful. I had never felt or needed anything so profoundly. One moment I was viewing the scene from my window seat, then suddenly, the crowd was parting, stepping aside, to let me through.

The circle of dancing women closed around me. The drum was my heartbeat, my blood, it spoke to me like a chorus of millions. My muscles were no longer my own, they belonged to the drum. Everything I thought, felt, heard, and did belonged to the drum. I lived only to dance. I moved my slight ten-year-old body in impossible ways—undulating chest, rotating hip, quick-stepping feet, revolution of the head, and delicate hand gestures. I danced until there was only silence.

Suddenly, I was a paper-thin image of myself, with the audience watching the drummers play and witnessing the child rippling feverishly in the centre. Her eyes were glossed over, and her lips were sealed into a secret smile, her expression shifting as the secret unfolded, portraying codes and messages only the initiated could interpret. Someone had placed the ceremonial tray upon her head, and she danced, sure-footed as a mountain goat, graceful as a ballerina. The child's chest no longer heaved up and down from exhaustion, but ebbed and flowed with the sea and the tropical air. The women bustled around, supporting her every gesture, fulfilling her every need...

Silently, silently, we communicated. Only the sustaining sound of the drum faded in and out of our consciousness, pounding out the terrifying rhythms, holding us captive in a place I did not want to be. I remember the taste of something bitter in my mouth, I felt tears on my face and drank in their saltiness. I felt frightened, helpless, yet serene and powerful.

At some point during the night I was finally set free to rejoin myself, and I ran for a place to hide, a place where I could weep and forget. I wanted to deny the experience, even to myself.

The feast lasted three days and three nights. The people danced ceaselessly, chanting and singing. Animal sacrifices were made and offered with praise to the supreme god and the deities. The tray with which I had danced was brought into the house, and each room was blessed with its sanctified water.

I, however, kept my distance.

It would be twenty-odd years before I began to unravel the secret messages of the women's chants and the sacred codes of the drums. It would take a lifetime to unfold the pages of my history and reclaim my ancestry. Along the way I discovered that I was denied access to the knowledge, beauty, and inspiration of my African ancestry. Patriarchal education had led me to believe that Africa was the "dark continent," devoid of contributions to civilization. I found out, instead, that Greece and Rome inherited their civilization from Africa. I learned that Africa was the cradle of civilization and the place where human life began. I learned of the horrors of the slave trade and the middle passage. And I wept again from the pain of five hundred years of British colonization and humiliation.

Gradually, I also began to see past the thicket of feelings and lies handed down through the generations, to realize and understand the deep insecurities black people face as we struggle to re-invent and reclaim ourselves. Eventually, I understood that denial of ourselves as Africans is the burden we inherit from chattel slavery. Like so many others I had made the mistake of rejecting my African culture, judging its worth through the ignorance of my own enslaved mind. I now look upon myself and my root culture without shame or fear. And as I yield to my spiritual urgings again, with great eagerness and joy, I know that everything I have experienced has granted me the means to recognize the many gifts and breakthroughs in the dance of my life. Finally, I am able to appreciate that my mother's Shango dance, the home in which

I was born, and the influence of my family and ancestral traditions are pivotal to all that I have—and will—become.

Bernadette Charles
Pierrefonds, Quebec

The transatlantic slave trade brought millions of Africans to the western hemisphere. Those who were dispersed throughout the Caribbean and in North and South American colonies met with Indigenous people, many of whose religious and cultural beliefs closely resembled their own. Christian indoctrination, however, was used to "humanize" and simultaneously subordinate the captives, and all slaves were required to Christianize. Over the centuries a dynamic religious syncretism developed, combining African, Christian, and Indigenous elements. These syncretistic customs took several forms, depending on the geographical, historical, and political climate in which they took root. Haiti, for example, became the home of Voudon (Voodoo); Santeria developed in Cuba and the Rastafaria movement, in Jamaica. In Trinidad and Grenada, Shango and Spiritual Baptists held sway.

Afro-Caribbean traditions defy classification as a unified movement. There are, however, shared characteristics which may include divination, possession, healing, ecstatic worship, honouring ancestors, and propitiating deities; music and dance figure profoundly. These powerful, creative traditions have been targets of ridicule and suppression, and dominant Western religions have contributed to their devaluation. Scant archeological and historical information, combined with Western theological values, resulted in the notion that African-based religions were inferior. Only now are the complexity of ancient African civilizations and the vitality of their legacies gaining ground in the study of religion.

Afro-Caribbean traditions flourish among a wealth of autonomous congregations and practitioners. There are no single governing bodies, nor are there statistics regarding how extensively practised such traditions are in Canada. Toronto and Montreal, however, harbour large Caribbean communities, where Spiritual Baptists, Voodoun, Shango, and a variety of Afro-Christian denominations continue to thrive.

PRECIOUS KNOWLEDGE,
SACRED DANCE

*In Madras I sat in on an ordinary lesson hour in the
school of one of the great dancers in this [Bharata
Natyam] tradition, Bala Saraswati. The monsoon
roared down on the palm leaf roof, a wood Victorian
clock stood on the table, a new bicycle was propped up
in one corner, a local Brahmin camped
inconspicuously in another, in a third there were
rough chairs piled up to the rough timber rafters. The
instructress and her musicians squatted on the
ground, courteous to their visitors but at once lost
again in their tasks. Nothing could have seem less arty,
more genuine. But after all, it was a school, and the*

best of her pupils—her dancing a sheer delight—was
the daughter of the local professor of Sanskrit.

John Holloway *The Colours of Clarity*

The young girl in Holloway's sketch grew into an outstanding performance artist and teacher who now inspires her own pupils to excellence, far from her native Madras. Priyamvada Sankar's dedication to her art and devotion to her students are firmly rooted in her identity as an orthodox Hindu; the fulfillment of her duties as artist, guru, wife, mother, lecturer, and businesswoman confirms this deep religious sensibility.

I first met Priyamvada at the Durga temple in Montreal, where she donates her time teaching. Drawn by her sheer radiance and intrigued at how she transformed a roomful of energetic girls into elegant dancers, I approached Priyamvada to learn more:

It is said that in the golden age, the first age in Hindu mythology, Brahma, creator of the universe, was asked by the Devas (divine beings) to create an art form which would be pleasing to the gods. So Brahma took something from each of the Vedas. From the Rig Veda he took the written word and from the Yajur Veda, the presentation. From the Sama Veda he took the music and from the Atharva Veda, the emotions or sentiments. And Brahma called this creation Natya Veda, for *natya* means dance. But now he needed someone to perform this beautiful art, so Shiva took the task upon himself as Nataraja, and he performed the first cosmic dance, the Dance of Supreme Bliss.

When Nataraja performed this dance, the whole universe saw it. And Bharata, the sage, a devotee of Shiva, learned the dance as well. He and his sons then taught it to the divine beings, including the *apsaras*, women who were very artistic and very beautiful. And it is believed that through them the dance was handed down to women on earth. So this dance, which is highly symbolic and expresses the joy of life, was given to humans by God himself.

We believe that our Bharata Natyam has come down from a particular dance, Lasya, performed by Shiva's wife, Parvati. About four hundred years ago in South India in the royal courts of Tanjore, whose kings were great patrons of the arts, there were four dance masters who codified the present dance form. They set down the rules and regulations as to how to teach this dance and how to perform it. And from these masters there evolved several families which developed different schools of dance. My dance master and teacher were both direct descendants of these very first masters; so I too became a direct descendant and had the gift of receiving my education from these two illustrious people. And the additional bonus in my life was my father, who was as dedicated to this art form as any artist.

I began dancing when I was five years old. At that age I didn't know I was interested in dance, but my father watched me and believed I had talent, so he put me under the tutelage of my teacher, the renowned Bala Saraswati. At once I became intensely devoted to the art. I had such a passion for it, even as a child, that I went there seven days a week and cried if I had to miss a class.

At that time it was rare for a Hindu Brahmin girl to learn Bharata Natyam because even though the dance originated in the temple and was developed by deva-dasis, the dance had fallen into disrepute. Deva-dasis were female dancers and singers who dedicated themselves to the temple and performed worship through these art forms; so the dance had a beautiful beginning. But after British rule, when the kings and temples lost their power, these women lost their source of income, and in order to make a living, they had to seek support from wealthy patrons. These arrangements corrupted the art, and it lost its sanctity. It took a lot of courageous men and women to restore the dance to its original eminence. My father was one of those people. He saw the dance as a beautiful art form and he saw my teacher as a genius. He helped revive the true glory of the art by setting up a school in the Madras Music Academy to train young girls. And I was its very first student.

Then at the age of twenty-one I got married. Marriage was a big step for me because I had never envisioned leaving my home and family, and because I had worked so closely with my father. Apart from my music and dance teachers, my father was my other guru. I learned from him not only the ancient Sanskrit language but also the tradition and culture. He was at once a Sanskrit scholar and poet; an expert in Indian music, dance, and drama; and a prolific writer in English, Tamil, and Sanskrit. I was very close to him, and because of that I was immersed in a world of dance, music, lectures, books, painting, temples, and rituals. It was amazing to have that kind of knowledge around me, and when I was eight or nine years old, I realized I was blessed with someone very special from whom I should learn as much as I could.

So when the time came for me to marry, my parents started looking for a suitable young man. People would say, "Well, your daughter can dance all she wants before marriage because she may not have a chance to do it afterwards." "There is no way I'm getting married under that condition," I said. I knew dance was with me for life, a prized possession that I wasn't going to give up, even for the finest husband. Knowing that, my father looked for a man who would appreciate my art and, like himself, be both a scholar and a good provider.

It so happened that the first young man my father arranged for me to meet was the right one. The only thing was, he was living in the West. I thought, "Oh no, I have to go to Canada?" I wasn't anticipating that. I would lose my family and my home; I would be completely alienated from my music and dance teachers. I could not bear to think of it. But my father told me to keep an open mind. "Just because it is the West," he stressed, "doesn't mean you are going to give up everything. You may have more opportunities. You may teach there, and you may be able to make a name for yourself. Your husband has lived in the West, so he has a better outlook than some here who may not approve of your intense dedication to dance."

Sometime after my marriage, I arrived in Canada, and my first fear was, "What would I do if I could not practise my dance or continue my culture?" So I came armed with things to help me feel at home: pictures of deities, icons, art work, and other items of worship. I had all these little prayer books, things which were essential to keep our faith.

And when I came to Montreal, I brought with me not only my religious items but also tapes of my music, my dance costumes, and fine jewellery. Fortunately, it was the year after Expo '67, and the Indian pavillion had had some dancers, so I made contact with them. But it was so difficult to make people here aware of my art, since there was no knowledge of Hindu culture or Hindu dance. I was used to performing for two hours at a time, and here I was with people who only had fifteen or twenty minutes during a community function. So I practised in our small apartment, but that disturbed the other tenants. At times I was so downhearted, I used to think, "Why did I come to this place?"

Naturally, I had come because I was no longer solely a dancer; I was also a married woman who loved her husband, and I took my new duties very seriously. This too was a reflection of my orthodox upbringing. Being a dutiful wife and mother gave me great satisfaction, but it also meant I had to juggle a great many things. Besides supporting my husband's career and helping him fulfill his duties to his family, I was raising our two sons, performing in the community, and starting a new dance school. And in the midst of all this my father died suddenly. It was then I realized that the responsibility now fell to me to promote the dance as fully as possible. Only then could I rightfully honour my father's work and preserve his legacy and spirit.

So slowly, slowly, things developed; it took until 1980 for the school to become fully recognized. Starting with Montreal's very first Bharata Natyam graduation performance, followed by several others over the years, and with an impressive list of performances, benefit concerts, conferences, demonstrations, and so on, gradually, the school gained renown for maintaining the art in its purest original form. And in 1994 we celebrated the dance school's twenty-fifth anniversary. That was a real triumph for my family and my students. So many people had helped me become established; the celebration allowed me to honour them also.

Now in addition to the school I also teach at two temples. This arrangement allows families, many of whom are immigrants and refugees torn away from their culture and their homelands, to allow their daughters to learn the ancient aspects of Hinduism. Since the dance is rooted in our sacred texts and mythology, the children not only learn these powerful, enchanting stories, they learn a sublime art form as well.

And this knowledge is very important to these people because it helps them maintain their cultural and religious identity. It's very difficult to change totally when you're born in a certain culture and brought up in a certain way. It's hard. I have learned to accomodate, and now I feel perfectly at home here. But I understand very well the struggle to maintain a staunch religious practice. And I know that without the dance I would be lost—it is my culture, my religion, and my tradition. Basically, I'm a religious person, and this sacred art has become intensely important to me. Over the years the dance has become a form of meditation and another avenue for my prayer.

Of course, I am deeply fortunate to be able to combine both my professional and my religious life. And my efforts are in great part supported by my loving family, whose encouragement and appreciation have inspired me to continue my work. But the other reason I have survived as a dancer is because of hope, the aspiration that I share the dance with people here, and that by my teaching the purity and integrity of my dance tradition will continue into the next generation.

For me, teaching is a dharma in which I am trying to transform another human being into a vibrant dancer. It's difficult for children to understand the value of this art. They have to experience it slowly. Not all children become devoted to the dance, of course, but the ones that do become more and more involved until, by the time they graduate, their dedication and fascination are complete. You can see it in their eyes—it's like magic, an energy which possesses them. It is a beautiful thing, this relationship, because I experience what that child is feeling all over again, and she, in turn, is drawing the feeling from me.

Dance has been a very important aspect of my life, and as I grow older, I realize I won't be able to do it forever. But I want to do it for as long as possible. It's a passion that doesn't lessen with the years. There is immense satisfaction in the feeling that I have created so many good students and have the privilege of teaching so many capable, strong, and loving young women. When I teach in the temple, for instance, I don't want to miss even one class. The children are so eager and the parents are so eager, I want to give them my best. My classes mean so much to me because the knowledge, which is so precious to me, I, in turn, am trying to give to a child. This then is my ritual and my lifestyle. The traditional Hindu woman regards even the act of cooking as a ritual. She does it for her family, and that is how she cares for them. So for an artist, training a child in divine dance is another kind of ritual—making her realize the value of it, training her to respect and develop her own faith and religious feeling. All this is my responsibility, my dharma. My salvation is through that. And my joy.

Priyamvada Sankar
Brossard, Quebec

Underlying the complex interplay of philosophical insights and pluralistic traditions in Hinduism is the belief that there is but one god with many names. Since the divine is limitless and beyond human comprehension, God can assume a multiplicity of forms. The worship of many deities is sometimes erroneously equated with polytheism. In fact, Hindus worship a single God through serving a variety of deities. Among these, three are chief and are worshipped by millions of Hindus worldwide. Brahma, the creator, is responsible for both nature and society. Vishnu, the preserver, periodically manifests in various forms (avatars) to protect goodness and destroy evil. Avatars such as Rama, Krishna, Gautama the Buddha, and so on appear on earth to help humanity in trying times. Finally, there is Shiva, the destroyer, the most popular of the gods. Shiva wields power over death, disease, and reproduction; Shiva as Nataraja is the god of dance.

Devotional practices and teachings are transmitted through gurus. The more sophisticated or esoteric of these paths are not for everyone, however, and Hinduism has adapted to meet the needs of people of all kinds at every social level. The primary concern of most Hindus is less philosophical than pragmatic—how does one live life appropriately? The answer lies in dharma, fulfilling one's sacred duty. The four goals of life, divisions of labour, and the caste system are all interpreted in light of the desire to order things in a proper and fitting manner. Thus, all aspects of personal, social, and political life are addressed within Hinduism's ancient, comprehensive approach.

Throughout its long history Hinduism has had innumerable ups and downs. It has survived fierce attacks, embraced friendly beliefs, and has continued to inspire every faithful follower. Today Hinduism not only stands for ancient beliefs and worship but has also combined with social concern to lead people with stronger spiritual unity. This influence is so strong that even followers living outside India are deeply motivated by Hinduism's teachings and practice.

WAITING FOR MORNING:
Artist and Icon

The story of Russian iconographer, Tatiana Vartanova, is every bit as remarkable as the saints' tales she recounts with great affection. As a young artist in the grip of political intrigue, Tatiana found herself drawn to religion, the very thing communism tried to suppress.

Reared in a one-room flat on the outskirts of Moscow, Tatiana had little contact with Russia's rich spiritual heritage until a fellow art student at university invited her to paint the interior of a rural church—an act for which they were seized and interrogated by local police. After marriage and the birth of her first child Tatiana and her husband moved abroad. Failed attempts at defection drove the young family back to Moscow, where they were imprisoned by the KGB and ostracized by political dissidents who considered the couple too dangerous to associate with. Religious dissidents, however, befriended the couple and in 1977 arranged for Tatiana to work in Orthodoxy's holiest shrine, the Moscow Patriarchal Epiphany Cathedral. Eventually appointed the cathedral's principal artist, Tatiana directed the ambitious restoration of its vast collection of icons in honour of Russian Christianity's millennial celebrations in 1988.

Tatiana Vartanova immigrated to Canada in 1990 and is one of only two hundred iconographers nationwide. The following account is based on an interview with Tatiana at her home in Ottawa.

I am a theatre artist by profession, but I didn't work in the theatre. It was interesting to study, but it's not in my nature. I like to work alone. That's why I began to study commercial art, which I worked at successfully until I went to Egypt with my husband. After that I lost everything. We moved from Egypt to the USA, and when I returned to Moscow, the government denied me work. That's when I met religious people, dissidents who helped me, and they recommended me to the cathedral.

There were thousands of icons in the cathedral. The main iconostasis alone had ninety icons, many of which needed cleaning and restoration. But of course, I didn't know how to paint icons so I had to study with monks who did. We didn't have a special university for this, nothing; only certain people who could paint like that.

But you know, when I was a teenager, I was already interested in icons, and I tried making them on my own. I took a simple wood panel and put nails and wire on it and plaster for the walls. It was very crude. But I wanted to know how icons were made. I don't know why. My soul was interested in how they were done. Of course, I seldom saw real icons, only when I was at church with my mother. And my grandparents in the Ukraine had primitive icons in their home. I also saw icons in art books, and I experimented a little. But after that I left them alone until my time in the church.

My first real contact with religion came when I was studying art at university. My friend, Sasha, had brothers who were priests, and sometimes I borrowed their books or saw religious articles in their apartment. It was the smell, especially, a special smell from all the icons and the books that affected me. That and what the priests wore. All this was fantastic. Now times have changed, but in the late sixties and early seventies we couldn't see people like that, and it was like a fairy tale.

Once my husband and I returned to Moscow from abroad, our lives were very restricted, very difficult. No one felt safe relating to us, and we became very isolated. It was priests and religious dissidents who reached out to us. I began to listen to their lectures and attend churches. And after the liturgy we had dinners, and I listened to what people spoke about. And I began to think about religion every day. I also began to read about it, and every day I became more and more interested.

Of course, in those days it was hard for churches, not so much for the cathedral because it was a government place, a showpiece for foreigners. Our work there was official, and we were well paid. But in other churches life was difficult. Vandals would try to destroy things. I might be having dinner with a priest, and someone would throw a stone at the window.

But even at the cathedral we had trouble. One time we had a lot of guests who wanted to see the Easter liturgy because it was so fantastic, with many bishops and choirs. So many people wanted to see it, we had to have tickets; only six thousand could be admitted. A friend asked me to help his daughter because they didn't have a ticket. And I said I would, of course. There were big fences around the cathedral and police patrols to keep order. And when I went out behind the fence to meet her, and we turned to go inside, the police officer said "No, you can't go in."

And I said "How can that be? You saw, just now, that I came out of the cathedral. I work there, and now you won't allow me to enter? That's impossible."

And he said "I don't know. You can't."

"See that small tower?" I said. "It is my workshop." (When I had a lot of work, I practically lived in the cathedral, and my mother took care of my children at home.) "See the light there?" I told him. "I left my radiator on for warmth. And an electric heater. And if a fire starts, you will be responsible. Give me your name; I will write it down. And you will be responsible." That scared him, so he let me go.

Of course, I also met many miraculous people. In 1981 a very special person came to the cathedral, a mathematician. This woman left her post in mathematics to come to the church. She wanted to be there so much, she agreed to come and clean the floors. She was a very unusual person, very strong in her beliefs. I learned a lot from her. I saw how she believed, how she hoped, how she was in contact with God. And what happened after that was a miracle, absolutely. Here she was so sick—she had breast cancer— and the doctors couldn't help her; it was too late for that. And she hoped and prayed, and the tumour disappeared; it shrank and disappeared. And she is still living, even now.

Many miraculous things happened with this woman's family, which she told me about. She had one relative who had killed himself. Suicide, she said, is very bad for the whole family, especially the children. And she had many dreams about this person—he was in a very dark place, a hard place, and she began to pray for him. And in time she saw him in a dream, and he was very happy and bright. And she felt something light, something easy, and peaceful in her soul. She became very quiet about him. "Now I am happy for him; his punishment is over," she told me. Each lunch time I went to her place after she had washed the floor. That's when we spoke, and she told me this.

So in the cathedral I was surrounded by these kinds of stories. I heard many stories from people, and they affected me deeply. Now I am sure that I too am not alone in any difficulty. I have my friend; I have my God. He is my best love; I don't know how else to say it. I am not alone. Always I am with him. I can even speak with him sometimes when I am working because I feel him with me. I don't see him, but he is near me always. I'm not rich spiritually. I have to study and I have to work with myself. I am not ideal, far from it. But I know one thing: I love him and I am not alone.

I have a special feeling for two Greek saints especially: Saint Panteleimon, who was a healer, and Saint Trifon. My grandfather was Greek. Maybe that's why I feel for them. Often, I asked Saint Panteleimon to help when someone from my family was sick. He always helped. Always. And I feel him very close.

But it isn't always so simple.

We have a wonderful saint, a Russian, Saint Seraphim Sarovsky, who lived in the nineteenth century. All Russia loves him. All people love him, and he performs many miracles.

His icon, of course, was in our cathedral. And very often I went near him but I was disturbed because I knew this was a great saint, but I couldn't feel him. I couldn't. It was very upsetting. I knew his life, I knew his story, but I felt nothing for him. It was terrible. And I knew too that he was a patron of young women, and I have two daughters. Why couldn't I feel him? I tried to pray to him. Nothing.

After we came to Canada, I had a problem with my children, and I decided to pray to Saint Seraphim for help. I had to pray to him because who could help me? By this time I was divorced, a single mother with two girls, completely on my own in a strange country. Of course, I can speak with God, but when I need help very often I ask saints because they were human, sinners like us. And I decided to read his *akathist* (prayer) every day for a whole year. Every evening, every day, I read it. And thank God, I had no problems with my children. Nothing bad happened to them.

After that my friend in Moscow who is also an artist went to Saint Seraphim's shrine, where his relics are kept. My friend worked there and helped the nuns, and they told him, "You have helped us a lot. We know you have people you are close to, and if you write down their names, we will pray for them forever." And he wrote my name and my daughters' names. And now the nuns pray for us, near Saint Seraphim's relics. It's a miracle because at one time I couldn't feel that saint at all.

It's very hard to describe Seraphim in English. What I can say is that he could love all people. He had so much love for people, he loved everyone. Once a criminal heard about Seraphim and decided to speak with him. The criminal went to Seraphim's place, and when he saw the man, Seraphim called out, "Hello, my love. I am very glad to meet you."

"No, it can't be," the man said. "You know I am a murderer. I am a criminal."

"It doesn't matter," Seraphim answered him. "Hello again, my love." And he called out the man's name. And after that the man felt so much love, he could not go back to his old ways. He became a good person. He changed because of a few words. Because of Seraphim.

Stories like this are very rich, very important. I have to know such stories before I can paint about someone. Now, of course, I also know about theology and the rules for iconography, the traditions for depicting saints, the Virgin, and Jesus Christ. And before painting, I think about these things. If I don't know something, I do research. But I have to know the story of this person before I can paint.

Of course, I can also look at historical icons that were painted in earlier centuries to see what I like and what I don't. I like to paint trees and architecture. I love to paint a lot of details, and I can choose details from each century.

All this is preparation. But when the time comes to paint, the icon lives in me. It's like when you read a book. When you read a book, you live with that story. And when I paint, I live in my icon. And when I am very interested in the details or I want to see how something turned out, I dream that morning will come soon, so that I can continue my painting. Every evening I wait for morning to come.

Each time I paint, it's different. Painting the face, especially, is difficult because I have to have more energy and be very careful. I have to be strong, and each time I have to feel something about the person I am painting. This is difficult because a saint is not like us. That person is special, and after all, I am a very small person, very simple. But I try to concentrate for one or two days, and usually on the third day I feel ready. Then I can paint.

Every morning I pray; I cannot even eat until I pray. I pray every evening too, but especially in the morning. I can do nothing without prayer. And before I paint, I always ask the saint to help me. Sometimes, when I do something that is not quite right, it disturbs me. It makes me suffer. Then I can't paint; especially the face of Jesus Christ—I just cannot paint it. I have to go to confession and receive Communion, and after that I can resume painting. Then I am a little better for a few days, at least during the period of painting the face! I cannot be always be perfect; I realize that.

And during hard times I know that things are difficult, but I know also that they will pass. There will come another time, and God will spoil me.

Sometimes people feel something special for me because I paint icons. I don't know why this is. Once at a university concert a woman asked me what I do and I said, "I paint icons." And she said, "Oh, let me touch you." I don't know why people do this; I don't feel special. I am only an instrument. God does everything through my right hand. He does everything. All I do is paint.

Tatiana Vartanova
Ottawa, Ontario

In Eastern Orthodox Christianity icons (from the Greek, *eikon*, for image) are sacred paintings depicting holy figures in highly stylized, symbolic form. Icons were at the centre of the Iconoclastic controversy in the eighth and ninth centuries that led to pronounced differences between Eastern and Western Christian art. While the West encourages pictorial representation of biblical events and doctrine, Eastern churches stress art's liturgical function.

The icon strives to represent an unseen reality and is the focus of prayerful veneration. The creation of genuine icons is an elaborate endeavour that can take several months, calling for a disciplined spiritual and artistic life on the part of the painter. Prayer, fasting, and an in-depth knowledge of the theological conventions governing the design and formation of icons are essential steps in the process. For that reason, icon painting may be regarded as a religious act.

Eastern Orthodoxy traces its origin and authority directly to the teachings of Christ and the apostles. Orthodoxy in Russia was proclaimed the official faith in 988. In the fourteenth century the church became independent of Greek Orthodoxy, and leadership shifted to Moscow. The patriarchate of Moscow was established in 1589, was subsequently abolished by Peter the Great, and was re-established in 1917. Communism, however, banned all religious expression. Decades of hostility began to lift with glasnost and perestroika, and the church's revitalization after persecution and suppression has led to a strong resurgence in piety.

JOURNEY TO THE GODDESS:
Alive, at Newgrange

In Ireland the world of ordinary reality exists side by side with the world of spirit. Both recognize and honour the presence of the other. The island itself is steeped in the mystery of ancient tribes that once inhabited the land. Christianity has learned to accept the worlds of the little people and the land of Tir na nOg. A stop at Saint Patrick's Cathedral must be followed by a visit to the Hill of Tara to honour the heritage of both Christian and pagan cultures. Each god and goddess has its own place, with sacred sites and offerings.

History tells us that before the land was inhabited by Celts, Ireland was invaded by other tribes. In a time long ago the land of Erin was overtaken by a tribe from Greece, the tribe of the goddess Danu. The Tuatha Dé Danaan, the people of light, were a confederacy, in which kingship was determined by matrilineal succession. The invaders were depicted as accomplished soothsayers and necromancers, blessed with great powers that enabled them to quell storms, cure diseases, work in metals, and foretell the future. Tribal leaders and bards forged magical weapons and were known, on occasion, to raise the dead. The tribe was also renowned for its supernatural powers, held by virtue of the *lia fáil* or stone of destiny. The tribe of the goddess Danu remained in Ireland for many years until displaced by the Milesians and Gaelic tribes later to be known as the Celts.

The Tuatha Dé Danaan fought the Milesians and, upon losing the battle, were said to have disappeared. Folklore tells us the conquered did not leave Ireland but sought to remain in their beloved land by retreating into the hills and mounds until such times as they were called to return to their rightful place. Their presence in Ireland is acknowledged still; they are "the little people," the children of light.

Stage I

Returning to this ancient land,
I begin my journey
It is a long journey
One that will take a lifetime to complete
I come to this place in search of my soul
My mirror reflection
I seek the Goddess Danu
I seek the light
My heart pounds with anticipation
The same questions reverberate in my head
Over and over again
Who am I?
Where did I come from?
Who are my people?
Am I an alien being?
From the tribe of the Tuatha Dé Danaan
Did I once inhabit this place?

Am I but a spirit
In human form?
Experiencing this material world for insight?
My senses are awake
When I am in this magical place
Every fibre of my body
Sings with joy
Feel the earth beneath my feet
Taste the wind
Hear the words of birds
I fly with them, up, up
Over, over, the mountains
To the North, to the South
To the *Grianan of Aileach*
I am the earth,
I am the sky
I am immortal
There are no answers,
Only more questions

Stage II

Quiet, quiet, still still
Words cannot bring answers
Words bring confusion
Silence, silence
Lay down, lay down
Sleep, sleep
The Mother enfolds me
Dream, dream
Quiet, dream sleep,
fly, fly
Over land, over sea
Up, up
Rising into
ether air
To awake, to awake
to begin again
To renew the journey

Stage III

Throughout this ancient land
There remain
Elements of a past
Familiar places
Familiar tastes
Sounds of tinkling bells
In the inner heart
My human body responds
to the essence
Here I am truly alive
Go, go,
back to the ancient mounds
Newgrange, Tara
Get off the bus,
Leave the bus behind
Lay in the arms of Mother Earth
For here, here is where
Her heart remains
She is caught between the worlds
Like I
The struggle of spirit
and human form
Wanting to be free,
But held back by those
Who do not believe
in her existence

Stage IV

Awake, awake
Kind Mother
I kneel at your fountains
and streams
I need no altar
Nor church spire
For I have the
Blue sky overhead
for my mantle

Stage V

Enter the cave of
wonderment
Enter the stone passage
Feel every fibre of the human body
Resonate to the energy
held between the stones
The passage is narrow
and cold
Breathe, breathe the
life breath
Release, release the air
in lungs exploding
Aha, aha, we enter
the cave of life
We enter the birthing room
We are alive and the
cycle begins again
Birth, death, life
There are no answers
Only more questions

Stage VI

Inside the birthing room
I gather up my human clothes
To begin the journey
back to reality
For I understand
that I am from
The ancient Tribe of the
Goddess Danu
The Children of Love
Here, to bring light
To those who question
And do not believe
Sleep, sleep
Quiet, Quiet

The story ends
The circle
Begins again

Ann Brennan
Bath, New Brunswick

Many consider the search for the Goddess a recent phenomenon in response to the patriarchal, monotheistic nature of Western religion. Yet veneration of the divine feminine is not restricted to New Age or feminist consciousness. Female deities in Hinduism, Tara in Buddhism, and European Christianity's black madonnas are ample evidence that sacred female imagery has long permeated world religions.

In fact, images of the Divine Mother once flourished in the Western religious imagination. So say those who insist that our lack of knowledge about her is due to suppression by male-dominated religions. The re-emergence of her veneration is paralleled by striking, if controversial, arguments that certain archaeological finds are direct evidence of goddess worship and/or ancient female-centred cultures.

This analysis questions how history itself is understood. The notion that Western civilization is rooted in the "high" civilizations of Egypt, Greece, and Mesoptamia ignores significant artistic and architectural legacies from prehistory. Proponents argue that the ancient remains of caves, sacred mounds, kivas, and cliff dwellings from the paleolithic and neolithic eras are not only replete with female symbolism but that they verify the dominance of matriarchies spanning nearly thirty thousand years (from 25,000 BCE). Once the destination of pilgrims and soothsayers, these sacred sites are still venerated by those who wish to experience the divine feminine's sacred power. Newgrange Passage Mound in Ireland is one of these sites.

By some measures there is little proof of ancient matriarchal societies that thrived without war or hierarchical political structures. Advocates, however, are not deterred by skepticism. While further investigation is needed, countless devotees (over 100,000 in North America alone) of this growing spirituality movement are ensuring that, one way or the other, the Goddess is remembered.

TKNU O'KOM (THE SWEATLODGE):
A place to pray

Don't turn the pages
The heart lays bare
The story of one's life must be told
I am gone—
The word will be all there is

Mi'kmaq elder and renaissance poet, Rita Joe, was orphaned in childhood and reared in foster homes and residential school. This upheaval resulted in the loss of precious cultural knowledge and skills which Rita Joe worked hard to recover later in life, primarily through writing. Her popular column for *The Micmac News* drew on stories she gleaned from elders, and the old ways have been eloquently affirmed in her poems, books, and songs.

Rita Joe went on to become a distinguished writer and educator whose works touch people the world over. Her message about the beauty, wisdom, and integrity of Native cultures is aimed at overturning negative images and stereotypes. Listen, she says, to "our wampum, our stone writings, our words." Here Rita Joe invites us to witness her own story as she walks us through the ancient prayer form of the sweatlodge.

Tknu O'Kom

I am reasoning something for which
there is no name
I ask many people, it was quieted long ago.
It is about a sweatlodge, a place where
we sweat.
Where we pray, sing and converse with
Niskam
Tknu is sweat, *O'kom* is lodge.
I also learned it was called *alasutmo'kom*
A place where you pray.
Today we call church *alasutmo'kom*
Alasutman is to pray,
also done since long ago.
My reasoning draws a lot of questions
The word *alasutman* has been around
for centuries.
That means we had spiritual values long
before you came.
Kisulkip we knew, the one who made us.
Wejiwuli Niskam, the Holy Spirit.
On and on my fame.
That is the reason I write—
The image you created, I turn around.

Let me tell about my first sweatlodge ceremony. We were all female, the thirteen of us—one child and twelve grown women. And I was the eldest. A women's sweatlodge is more powerful than the men's. Some of us had never done the sweatlodge before, and we were fascinated to find out what would happen. There is nobody to teach us what was traditionally done. We have had to discover it ourselves by observing and listening to others and by doing it ourselves.

I was told to go in first because I was the oldest; the others would follow according to their age. So I crawled into the enclosed area of the sweatlodge on my hands and knees and asked out loud for my ancestors to help me. The enclosure is not even as tall as I am; I could not stand up in it, but it is big and round and there is a pit in the middle for the heated rocks. When we were all inside, the door was closed and we started the first formation. Each formation lasts twenty minutes, and after each one another rock is put into the lodge, and we are given a little water to drink. I happened to be sitting alongside Donna Augustine from Big Cove, New Brunswick, who was leading the sweatlodge. She was the first to speak, asking for spiritual help.

The stones in the pit were very, very hot, and oh, I was sweating. It was like a very hot sauna. I was doing my thing in my mind, not talking out loud but to myself, in my own way, in a spiritual way. My eyes were closed, and I could hear the others speaking one by one, and I could hear something else as well. I didn't understand this other sound. It seemed like eagles' wings flapping; it was powerful. In my own explorations it was something that I was doing to myself; but at the same time, I knew that what I was hearing was not the same as the sound that I was making. I could not explain this, and I realized something spiritual was happening.

Finally, the door opened, and we were given a bit of water. In a few minutes another rock was placed in the pit. When the door opened, I couldn't wear my glasses because they had fogged over. You are not allowed to wear a watch or anything metal—not even a bra—because the metal will burn your skin. So I had a baggy old dress on, and the sweat was pouring off me. One of my daughters was sitting alongside me, and another daughter was sitting near the door. "Do you want to leave, Mom?" they kept asking.

"No, no," I said. I wanted all four formations. "Close the door." So we began the second formation—another twenty minutes. Again I could hear the sound, and something unusual began to happen. Without my thinking about it or doing anything to make it happen, my hand began to lift up and then drop, lift and drop. This happened four times before I finally said, "Leave me alone!" I was talking to the spirits that were doing this to me. Of course, I was perfectly safe; they were just telling me they were there. After that I had a feeling of great peace and goodness. I would ask a question in my mind, and immediately an answer would come to me.

When I finally came out of the lodge, I was still sweating. Everyone was soaking from sweat. I was looking around for my terrycloth robe to put over my baggy dress because I didn't want to get a chill, and I asked one of my daughters, "Do you know where my robe is?" She looked at me and said, "You're not wet!" I noticed for the first time that I was no longer soaked. I still do not know what happened because when I was inside the lodge, I could feel the sweat trickling down my back. I looked around and saw another woman who was also dry. But she did not notice me; she was too busy holding onto the way you feel when you come out of the sweat—when you come out, you feel pure.

Everybody was hugging me, but all the while I had the feeling of not wanting to touch anybody. It was a beautiful feeling of purification and spiritual force in my body.

> ...I must tell, my people say
> Together we must find a middle way
> Come and see how we live today
> Only then you'll know my nation well.
> Together, we find the wishing game
> That all people know each other well
> Together, we find the wishing game
> That in this country we live in peaceful ways...
> *Telimkik mta elu'li'oq*
> *Toqi-wejitu'k/na mowiomi*
> *Jukita'q na jik-qy-wi-nen*
> *Kisi-kjiji-wi-tes-nen na tujiw.*
> *Toqi kwilmnej na weloti*
> *Na msit wel-ik-ji-tul-tis-nu etuk*
> *Toqo kwilmnej na weloti*
> *Na tan wikik wel-am-atul-tis-nu.*
>
> from "The Wishing Game"
> ### Rita Joe
> ### Eskasoni, Cape Breton Island,
> ### Nova Scotia

Mi'kmaq were once the dominant maritime nation of northeastern North America and among the first Aboriginal peoples to come into contact with Europeans, perhaps as early as the fifteenth century. Traditionally a semi-nomadic people who moved between fishing villages in the summer and winter hunting sites inland, Mi'kmaq were renowned for a wide range of practical and artistic skills. Ongoing power struggles among Europeans for control of the eastern seaboard, however, brought conflict and disease and disrupted Mi'kmaq ways.

Today over twenty thousand Mi'kmaq live on and off reserves throughout New Brunswick, Prince Edward Island, Quebec, Newfoundland, and Nova Scotia. In recent years Mi'kmaq have launched sustained efforts to regain control of their financial resources, to establish self-government, and to reclaim traditional hunting and fishing rights. As with other Aboriginal peoples Mi'kmaq are addressing the crippling effects of acculturation—the root cause of so many social problems—through revitalizing traditional values.

Pride and cultural awareness have mitigated five hundred years of pressure to conform to non-Native norms, and a crucial part of this resistance is a strong spiritual base. Religion permeates all aspects of traditional Mi'kmaq life, everything from hunting to dreams to care for the sick. This core of sacred rituals and beliefs has continued despite the successful introduction of Christianity by French priests in the early 1600s. Perhaps the best known of these traditions are the stories of Glooscap (also Kluscap), trickster– transformer and hero, whose legends first made their way into North American popular culture over a hundred years ago.

KAUATIKUMAPEU:

The Man Who Married a Caribou

Stories lie at the heart of Innu culture. Storytelling is tied to life on the land and to the rhythm of the hunt, when long hours of confinement in tents are broken by the recitation of ancient tales. Matnen Benuen herself learned stories this way from her father and grandparents when she began making the seasonal trips to *nutshimit* (the country) with her family at the age of seven.

The following myth focuses on animals' and humans' intermarrying and on the interdependence of cultural and natural domains. Union between the man and the caribou god's daughter signifies both the material and the spiritual bond between Innu and the caribou, traditionally their source of life. Now, however, this bond is severely strained: "The only time I tell stories is when we are in *nutshimit*. There nothing is in the way; it's all open. It's too hard to do it in the community; there are too many distractions."

Matnen's poignant admission underscores the dissonance between a settled life and nomadism. In *nutshimit* knowledge of traditional skills ensures success over starvation; in settlements even the stories are marginalized.

"The Man Who Married a Caribou" was originally recounted by Matnen Benuen to her son in Innu in the fall of 1996 for a BBC radio project. Translation of the account has made possible its inclusion in this collection. In honour of the practice of letting a story speak for itself, the following account stands alone, without commentary.

A long time ago there were people called Innu. There was a young man and his parents, and one night they were almost ready to sleep. They were still up when the man's father said to his wife and son, "It's time for us to sleep; it's getting late." The man and his family were ready to sleep, and the young man lay down in the dark, and finally he fell asleep and had a dream.

As soon as it was daylight, everybody in the camp was up. They were already up before the sun rose. But the man slept late. His father said, "Get up now; the sun will be up soon," and the boy got up right away. The tent was already warm, and food and tea were ready for him. He ate and was ready to go out hunting for the day. His food and other things were already packed in his hunting bag. But before he left, he told his father that he had had a dream that night. He dreamt that a caribou had asked him to marry her, and he told his father his dream and then left with his bow and arrow and off he went.

As he walked, he climbed a mountian to look out over a lake, to check if he could see anything. And down below him he saw a huge herd of caribou. There were thousands on the ice. And as he went down toward the lake and got close to the shore, he saw one of the caribou stand up and move towards him. He got his bow ready to shoot the caribou, but the caribou spoke and said, "Don't shoot me. Listen to me." And the boy stood there with her and thought of the dream he had last night and said to himself, "My dream has come true."

And the caribou said to the boy, "You can marry me." But the boy said, "No! How can I marry you? I am a human and you are a caribou. If I marry you, I will go hungry and I will be cold and thirsty. I don't eat what a caribou eats and I will be left behind if the Innu chase you. And I will need a place to sleep." And so the boy still refused. But the caribou said, "You will not be hungry or cold or thirsty. You won't be left behind and you will have a place to sleep. We will take you everywhere we go and you will eat everything we eat." But the boy said "No!"

And the caribou said to the boy, "You see the caribou on the ice over there? If you come with me over there, you will feel as if you are in a tent, and the tent will be warm and there will be food ready." But still the boy refused. Then the caribou said, "If you don't agree to do what I have said and if you don't want to marry me, you will go home to your camp and you will get there, but as soon as you step into your father's tent, you will die right on the doorstep." The boy was nervous and afraid to go home. He feared that what the caribou had told him would happen. And so he finally agreed to do what the caribou said.

And Atikus (the young caribou) had been sent to listen to what was being said and see what happened. And the leader of the caribou had told Atikus that if the man agrees, you are to come running like a happy young caribou.

All the caribou on the ice were watching the man and the female caribou. All of a sudden, they saw Atikus running towards them, running like a happy young caribou. The caribou on the ice told each other that probably the man agreed to marry her, and they looked at each other and smiled as they saw the man and the caribou walk towards them.

As soon as the young man got to where the caribou were, he felt as if he had just walked into a tent. Everything was ready for him. And the boy said, "Can I go home and tell my father and my people?" And the caribou said no. The caribou told the young man, "If you marry me, you will never die. Your life will go on forever."

As the days went by, the father and mother worried about their son, and the father gathered all the men at the camp and told them to go and look for his son. Before everybody left, he told them that his son had had a dream about marrying a caribou, and the old man said probably the dream had come true. After they heard about this dream, all the men left the camp, and as they were walking, they saw footprints and they followed them to the lake. And they saw the tracks of a man and a caribou walking side by side.

Before they turned back, one of the men saw the young man's arrows leaning against a Maneik tree. So they took the arrows back to the camp and showed them to the old man. When the men got back to the camp, the old man asked one of them if they had found his son or any sign of him, and the man said, "No, but we found arrows that he left behind leaning against a big Maneik. And we saw two tracks walking together, a man's tracks and a caribou's tracks." And then the old man started to cry because he missed his son. And he cried for days and days.

One night the leader of the caribou told Atikus to go near the old man's camp and listen to hear if he were still crying, and Atikus returned and told the leader of the caribou that the old man was still crying.

Next day the old man told the hunters, "Go look for my son. If you see caribou, chase them. They might leave my son behind." So all the men went caribou hunting and they killed a small number of caribou, but not many. When they got back, they told the old man that they had killed some caribou, but the man was still crying, and there was nothing anyone could do to stop him.

Early the next morning the old man sent the men to look for his son again, and they left before sunrise. Again there was no sign of the old man's son, but once again they killed a few caribou and returned to camp before dark.

Again Atikus was sent to the camp to listen. When he returned, he told the leader of the caribou that the old man was a little bit better, sometimes crying and sometimes laughing. The caribou leader said, "I will give him more caribou, and probably he will become less unhappy."

On the third day a few men were sent out again to look for the young man again and again they found nothing of him, but they killed more caribou. Then they went back to the camp with the meat, and as soon as the old man saw that a lot of caribou had been killed, he started to laugh and was happy.

Once again Atikus was sent to see what was happening to the old man. And Atikus heard the old man laughing now, and he went back and told what he had heard. Then the leader of the caribou said, "That's enough for them; no more caribou. The people at the camp have a lot of caribou meat."

The next night the old man played his drum, and the people were dancing while he beat his drum and sang. And there was a *mukushan* (feast).

And that night, Atikus was sent again, and he saw the old man beating his drum and singing, and Atikus saw that he looked happy and went back to the caribou and told them that the old man was really happy now.

The man who married the caribou is *Kauatikumapeu*, and now he's the chief of the caribou. His herd is marked. It is the mark that he carries on his left ear.

On the last day the old caribou spoke to his son-in-law and told him that his father was happy now. And the leader of the caribou told his son-in-law, "You will stay healthy and you will be well looked after and you will never get old; you will always be young."

That's the end of the story of *Kauatikumapeu.*

as told by *Matnen Benuen*
Sheshatshit, Labrador

Canada's eastern subarctic is home to Innu, who have roamed the land for hundreds of years. Nitassinan is the Innu name for the territory that stretches from northeast Quebec to the Labrador peninsula. This territory was never ceded to the Canadian government, nor were treaties signed that justify appropriation of the land. Nevertheless, hunters and gatherers who once commanded vast distances on foot have now been relocated to settlements, where Innu life is disintegrating at an alarming rate.

Innu share certain affinities with other circumpolar peoples: life on the land is made possible by immense skill, ritual, and story; and animals, humans, and supernatural beings exist in intimate relationship with one another. Now, however, incursions into traditional territories are destroying hunting domains, burial sites, and trails, and threatening wildlife, while hydroelectric projects, mining, and low-level military flying have long since disrupted the harmonious balance between Innu and the environment. More insidious, however, are the relentless pressures of modernization, pressures that result in the gradual erosion of all that once gave order and meaning to life. Living in settlements has replaced self-sufficiency with an artificial security that manifests itself in addictions, suicide, and communal disintegration. Innu, however, are responding to degradation by working towards healing and self-determination. Along with political and legal activism, there are attempts at cultural resistance to assimilation. Such resistance, however, is made all the more difficult by the overwhelming presence of westernization on all fronts.

Storytelling is vital to maintaining and preserving Innu culture. Two forms of stories prevail. *Atanukan* feature mythical beings and contain truths that speak to the history and predicament of the Innu people. The other form is *Tipatshimun*, which can mean anything from history to news to tales within living memory such as what might be recalled by grandparents. *Atanukan*, however, are what introduce children to the pantheon of spirits and supernatural beings that animate their world. These myths contain cultural knowledge that shapes values and transmits a shared sensibility that prepares future generations for life.

ABOUT THE CONTRIBUTORS

Matnen Benuen was born in the village of Sheshatshit, near Goose Bay, Labrador. Her family, however, originated near Davis Inlet and was moved south in the early 1960s during resettlement. Matnen's knowledge of Innu ways is exceptional for someone of her generation, many of whom have lost touch with their heritage due to the destructive effects of acculturation. Matnen lives with her husband and seven children in Sheshatshit.

Heather Botting is an anthropologist whose academic interests have recently focused on the Wiccan religion. Since 1967 she has been the High Priestess of Coven Celeste, a British-based family tradition. She is active in public Wiccan rituals held in the Pacific Northwest as well as in rituals held under the auspices of the visiting clergy program within the federal penitentiary system. Heather works in the Centre for Studies in Religion & Society and is an instructor with the Anthropology Department at the University of Victoria.

Ann Brennan is a heritage artist who has delighted audiences across the country with her portrayal of Canadian heroes, notably Katherine Ryan (Klondike Kate). She has written prose, poetry, and historical plays; she is a founding member of the Writers Federation of New Brunswick, where she lives, and an originator of Irish-Canadian–First Nations cultural exchanges. The former teacher, businesswoman, community leader, and political acitivist is now enjoying the fruits of her labours in academe with a first-class honours BA in history.

Fredelle Brief is director of multifaith programming for Vision TV. An active participant in her Reconstructionist synagogue and in broader Jewish affairs, Fredelle is also married with three adult children. She has been involved in the peace movement and interfaith dialogue all her adult life. As past-president of the World Conference on Religion and Peace/Canada, Fredelle has participated in national and international conferences and has facilitated dialogue among groups with long histories of animosity.

Bernadette Charles is a mother, businesswoman, and dramatic poet who articulates her political and social concerns through a variety of media. Bernadette's passionate performances are lit by the quest to regain her African spiritual ancestry and to heal the debilitating effects that colonialism and chattel slavery have exerted on African religions and cultures. Born and raised in Grenada, Bernadette now makes her home with her husband and daughters in Pierrefonds, Quebec.

Louis Cormier hails from Rogersville, New Brunswick. After completing his BA, he moved to Montreal, where he has practised Buddhism for the past three decades under the tutelage of a wide range of masters. At present Louis is on the Montreal Interfaith Council. Past vice-president, administration, of the Buddhist Council of Canada, past-president of the Montreal Buddhist Council, and former CBC employee, Louis is pursuing graduate studies in religion at the Université du Québec à Montréal. He is married and has two daughters.

Soonoo Engineer was born in Mumbai (Bombay) and raised in Pune, India, where she also taught. After immigrating to Canada in 1958, Soonoo resumed her career, teaching English and history at the Vancouver Community College. A member of the Canadian Voice of Women, Women's International League for Peace, and president of the World Conference on Religion and Peace, Vancouver, she is also actively involved with interfaith organizations. Religion, philosophy, and writing poetry are her sustaining interests, and her teaching focus now is Eastern religions and culture.

Rolph Fernandes was born in Trinidad and joined the Franciscan Order in Montreal in 1957. Rolph studied meditation extensively in India with a variety of masters and lived in solitude at the foot of the Himalayas. Upon returning to Montreal, he became a pioneer in interfaith relations and a teacher of meditation. Having served on the Montreal Interfaith Council, Rolph now collaborates with Montreal's Inter-Cultural Institute and is a delegate for the Franciscan International Commission for Relations with Muslims.

Zohra Husaini is president of the Muslim Research Foundation, World Interfaith Education Association (Alberta) and an adjunct professor at the Centre for International Education and Development. With degrees in philosophy and sociology obtained in India, England, and Canada, Dr. Husaini writes and researches in a wide range of fields, including spirituality, women, and development. In addition, she is actively involved with multicultural, humanistic, and interfaith concerns. Edmonton has been home to Zohra Husaini for over twenty-five years.

Amir Hussain has been involved in interfaith work with the United Church for over a decade. Born in Pakistan, he came to Canada with his family when he was four years old. Amir grew up in Oakville, Ontario, and moved to Toronto in 1983. After graduating in psychology, he went on to pursue the academic study of religion. Currently, he is completing his PhD dissertation on the Muslim communities in Toronto and teaching religious studies at California State University, Northridge. Amir lives in exile in the San Fernando Valley.

Rita Joe has been appointed a member of the Privy Council and was awarded the Order of Canada and several honorary doctorates for her distinguished contributions to Canadian literature and culture. She began her writing career as a reporter for *The Micmac News,* and in 1978 *Poems of Rita Joe* was published to wide acclaim. She has since authored five books and attained international recognition for her role as Native renaissance poet. Rita Joe lives in Eskasoni, Cape Breton Island, Nova Scotia.

Deo Kernahan, a retired English teacher living in Etobicoke, Ontario, is now a researcher and contributor with Vision TV's flagship current affairs programme, *Skylight.* A director of Peace Fund Canada and vice-president of the Canadian Council of Hindus, Deo is also past-president of the World Conference on Religion for Peace. His articles on Hinduism have appeared in numerous publications.

Guru Raj Kaur Khalsa, whose name means "the princess (*kaur*) who establishes the rule of the Guru," became a Sikh at age twenty and one of the first ordained Sikh women in the West. She is a founding member and/or director of several key organizations, including Yoga West (where she teaches yoga and meditation), Sikh Youth of Canada, the Khalsa Credit Union (the first Sikh financial institution in the world), and the Khalsa Ladies Camp. Guru Raj owns and operates a graphic design business in Vancouver, where she lives with her husband and children.

Brian Kiely is a minister currently serving the Unitarian Church of Edmonton. Born in Montreal, Brian became an active Unitarian after moving to Toronto in 1980. He has served congregations in British Columbia and Ontario, sat on various denominational and professional committees, and is active in the choice-in-dying movement. In keeping with his recent writings on the importance of everyday spiritual practices, Brian can often be spied walking his dog along the North Saskatchewan riverbank.

Karen Laughlin began studying Taoist Tai Chi with Master Moy in Toronto in the late 1970s. Once she was initiated as a member of Fung Loy Kok Taoist Temple in 1981, Karen began teaching Taoism, Taoist Tai Chi, and other Taoist Arts and editing English translations of Taoist texts. She also serves as president of the Taoist Tai Chi Society of the United States. Dr. Laughlin is professor of English and Humanities at Florida State University, the author and editor of a variety of works on dramatic literature and theory and feminist aesthetics.

David Lawson is a writer and educator with a long-standing interest in Humanism. Originally from England he developed a distinguished literary and scholarly career that lured him to three continents—most recently Asia, where he taught for four years in China. Now retired, Dr. Lawson continues to publish poetry, novels, essays, and reviews, many of which reflect his background in history and philosophy of education. His work appears regularly in Humanist journals.

Brenda Acoose Morrison was raised on reserve in Sakimay, Saskatchewan. After an abusive upbringing she found herself at odds with the law and was incarcerated in Kingston's Prison for Women, where she then became the victim of further abuse. The notorious miscarriage of justice in Kingston in 1994 led to a federal inquiry and reform of the prison system for women in Canada. Okimaw Ohci Healing Lodge in Maple Creek, Saskatchewan, has changed Brenda's life, and she is now actively sought as a Lodge spokesperson.

Vastupal Parikh may have been the first Jain to settle in Canada, almost forty years ago. Upon his retiring from teaching chemistry Dr. Parikh's academic interests shifted to the theory of knowledge and its relationship to concepts in the ancient Jain scriptures; currently he is exploring the place of mystical insights in modern theories of knowledge. After having taught university for many years in British Columbia, Dr. Parikh moved with his family to Brampton, Ontario, where he is active in the Jain society and the United Way and is on the Public Library Board.

Leona Dueck Penner was born on a farm in Rosenhoff, Manitoba, in 1943, the fifth child in a Mennonite family which grew to eleven. For most of her adult life she has been involved with the Mennonite Central Committee (MCC)—a Christian service, development, and relief agency—in Winnipeg, Zambia, Swaziland, Botswana, and South Africa. Now retired from the workforce, she is writing and illustrating, leading a women's spiritual reflection group, and serving as worship leader at church.

Joyce Rappaport lives in Montreal, where she works as an editor, a writer, and an English teacher to new immigrants. Previously she was an assistant professor of English literature and writing at Chapman University in Sacramento, California. Joyce received her PhD in English literature at York University in 1984. Dr. Rappaport is married to a Conservative rabbi and is the mother of three sons.

Priyamvada Sankar immigrated to Quebec from her native Madras in 1968. A premier dance artist and teacher of Bharata Natyam—

the classical sacred dance of South India—Priyamvada is widely known for her artistic excellence in Carnatic music, and her knowledge of Sanskrit, Hindu culture, and tradition. A member of the Montreal Interfaith Council, Priyamvada is also active in the Hindu community, in arts and multicultural affairs, and in community development projects.

Shirlee Smith was the first black baby born in Women's College Hospital in Toronto. She and her twin brothers were raised by foster parents and were members of the First Baptist Church in Toronto, which had been built by former slaves. Shirlee became a Baha'i in 1964 while living in Bermuda. Shirlee is active in multicultural groups and as a counsellor to hard-of-hearing seniors. The tradition of storytelling is an integral part of her Black–Mohawk roots, and her stories reflect both her ancestral and spiritual heritage and her belief in Baha'u'llah, Prophet–Founder of the Baha'i faith.

Fred Louis Ulrich was born on the Great Plains to a German–First Nations family that had inherited Black Elk's vision. A Methodist minister before embracing Buddhism, Fred is now priest and leader of a Pure Land congregation in Winnipeg. He also counsels interfaith families and is active in Christian–Buddhist dialogue. A strong commitment to healing informs his translations of Buddhist texts for contemporary Western audiences. Having vowed to be a dharma teacher for a thousand lifetimes, Fred looks forward to retirement so he can focus on spiritual practice and enjoy his new grandchild.

Tatiana Vartanova was born in 1950 in Russia and trained as a theatre artist. Political peril shadowed her married life; she sought refuge with religious dissidents who found work for her in Russian Orthodoxy's holiest shrine, the Moscow cathedral. After learning the sacred art of icon painting from monks, Tatiana was appointed principal artist, responsible for thousands of icons. In 1990 she immigrated to Canada, where her work appears in museums, private collections, and churches. Tatiana makes her home with her two daughters in Ottawa.

About the Editor

Susan L. Scott is a writer, editor, and spiritual director. She works with faith communities, artists, scholars, and those who are marginalized or disabled, facilitating stories which would otherwise remain hidden or lost. Susan lives with her husband, Ron Grimes, and their two children in Waterloo, Ontario.

SOURCES

Blanchfield, Mike. "Lady of the Icon." *Ottawa Citizen*. 18 May 1997.

Brumble, David, III. *American Indian Autobiography*. Berkeley: University of California Press, 1988.

Chekhov Society of Ottawa. *Russian Canadians*. Ottawa: Borealis, 1983.

Faith in My Neighbour. Toronto: United Church Publishing House, 1994.

The HarperCollins Dictionary of Religion. San Francisco: HarperSanFrancisco, 1995.

Herberg, Edward N. *Ethnic Groups in Canada*. Scarborough: Nelson Canada, 1989.

Hoffman, John. *Faith-full Stories*. Toronto: United Church Publishing House, 1994.

Holloway, John. *The Colours of Clarity*. London: Routledge and Kegan Paul, 1964.

Klymasz, Robert B., ed. *The Icon in Canada*. Hull: Canadian Museum of Civilization, 1996.

Kornfield, Jack, and Christina Feldman. *Soul Food*. San Francisco: HarperSanFrancisco, 1996.

Langlais, Jacques, and David Rome. *Jews and French Quebecers*. Waterloo: Wilfrid Laurier University Press, 1991.

Matthews, Warren. *World Religions*. 2nd edition. St. Paul: West, 1995.

Monture-Angus, Patricia. *Thunder in my Soul*. Halifax: Fernwood, 1995.

Morrison, Bruce, and C. Roderick Wilson, eds. *Native Peoples*. 2nd edition. Toronto: Oxford University Press, 1995.

The Multifaith Calendar. 33 Arrowwood Place, Port Moody, BC, V3H 4J1. Telephone/fax: 604–469–1164.

Murphy, Terrence, and Roberto Perin, eds. *A Concise History of Christianity in Canada*. Toronto: Oxford University Press, 1996.

Nigosian, S. A. *World Faiths*. New York: St. Martin's, 1990.

The Oxford Dictionary of World Religions. Oxford: Oxford University Press, 1997.

Parkhill, Thomas C. *Weaving Ourselves into the Land*. Albany: SUNY, 1997.

Raghaven, V. *The Indian Heritage*. 4th edition. Basavangudi, India: The Indian Institute of World Culture, 1980.

Ross, Rupert. *Returning to the Teachings*. Toronto: Penguin, 1996.

Sharma, Arvind, ed. *Our Religions*. New York: HarperCollins, 1993.

Trigger, Bruce G., ed. *Handbook of North American Indians*. Washington: Smithsonian Institution, 1978.

Tzuk, Yogev. *A History of the Jews in Canada*. Montreal: TOR, 1993.

Vanier, Jean. *Becoming Human*. Toronto: Anansi, 1998.

Wadden, Marie. *Nitassinan*. Toronto: Douglas & McIntyre, 1996.

Wong, Hertha Dawn. *Sending My Heart Back Across the Years*. New York: Oxford University Press, 1992.

The companion
volume to

*STORIES IN MY
NEIGHBOUR'S FAITH!*

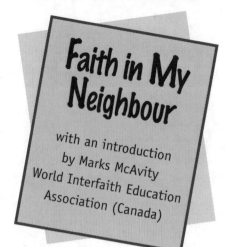

Faith in My Neighbour

with an introduction
by Marks McAvity
World Interfaith Education
Association (Canada)

Expand your multifaith library
with this contemporary survey
of Canada's world religions. Written in
the personal voices of community members, *Faith in My
Neighbour* explores the history, beliefs, symbols, and practices
of the many faiths in our country. An informative and readable
resource for all ages, *Faith in My Neighbour* explores the
following faith groups:

Baha'i	Judaism
Buddhism	Mormonism
Christianity	Native Spirituality
Hinduism	Sikhism
Humanism	Taoism
Islam	Unitarianism
Jainism	Wicca
Jehovah's Witnesses	Zoroastrianism

...the gift of understanding for all ages, cultures, and
faith groups!

Order today:
United Church Publishing House
1-800-288-7365
tel. 416-253-5456 or fax 416-253-1630
www.uccan.org

UCPH